SPAIN

BY LIZ SONNEBORN

Essential Library
An Imprint of Abdo Publishing
abdobooks.com

ABDOBOOKS.COM
Published by Abdo Publishing, a division of ABDO, PO Box 398166, Minneapolis, Minnesota 55439.

Printed in China.
052025
092025

THIS BOOK CONTAINS RECYCLED MATERIALS

Cover Photo: Shutterstock Images (town, pattern)
Interior Photos: Shutterstock Images, 4–5, 15, 16–17, 18 (globe), 20, 23, 27, 28–29, 30, 31, 36–37, 38–39, 41, 50–51, 54–55, 59, 61, 65, 66, 73, 74, 77, 78–79, 84, 88–89, 92–93, 101; Lorena Huerta/Shutterstock Images, 7; Alastair Wallace/Shutterstock Images, 9; Carlos Martin Diaz/Shutterstock Images, 10; Wesam Taleb/Shutterstock Images, 12; Red Line Editorial, 18 (Spain), 18 (Canary Islands); Lukasz Janyst/Shutterstock Images, 19; Francesca Sciarra/Shutterstock Images, 24; Jesus Giraldo Gutierrez/Shutterstock Images, 33; Carolyn Hill/Shutterstock Images, 34; Roman Belogorodov/Shutterstock Images, 42; Oleg Golovnev/Shutterstock Images, 44; Universal History Archive/Universal Images Group/Getty Images, 46; Oscar Gonzalez Fuentes/Shutterstock Images, 52, 71; Anek Soowannaphoom/Shutterstock Images, 57; John Silver/Shutterstock Images, 58; Julia Lavleis/Shutterstock Images, 62; Eduardo Parra/Europa Press News/Getty Images, 68–69; Juan Carlos Munoz/Shutterstock Images, 80; Alexey Fedorenko/Shutterstock Images, 83; Antonio Federico Puccio/Shutterstock Images, 87; Joan Bautista/Shutterstock Images, 90; Helena Garcia Huertas/Shutterstock Images, 97; Kaspars Grinvalds/Shutterstock Images, 98

Editor: Rebecca Higgins
Series Designer: Maggie Villaume

Library of Congress Control Number: 2024948605

PUBLISHER'S CATALOGING-IN-PUBLICATION DATA
Names: Sonneborn, Liz, author.
Title: Spain / by Liz Sonneborn
Description: Minneapolis, Minnesota: Abdo Publishing, 2026 | Series: Essential library of countries | Includes online resources and index.
Identifiers: ISBN 9781098297039 (lib. bdg.) | ISBN 9798384919551 (ebook)
Subjects: LCSH: Geography--Juvenile literature. | Spain--Juvenile literature. | Europe--Juvenile literature. | Spain--History--Juvenile literature.
Classification: DDC 946--dc23

CONTENTS

CHAPTER **ONE**

A TOUR OF SPAIN

Sitting in a rumbling subway car, Carlos can feel himself getting excited. Three days before, Carlos had flown with his dad, Javier, and his twin brother, Leo, from New York to Paris, France, where they visited with his Aunt Lucia. Early this morning, they got on another plane, this one touching down in Madrid, the capital of Spain.

For years, his father had promised to take Carlos and Leo on a tour through Spain when they turned 14, and now the day was finally here. Carlos was thrilled to visit the country. His dad was born and raised in Spain before moving to the United States.

When Carlos, Javier, and Leo reach Madrid's Sol Metro station, they join the crowd exiting the train.

Madrid became the capital of Spain in 1561.

As Carlos walks up the steps to leave the station, he looks up at the crystal-blue sky as a hot summer breeze warms his skin. At the top of the stairs is Puerta del Sol, a busy plaza considered to be the geographical center of the country. At the height of rush hour, many people are scrambling to board buses or make their way to Metro stations so they can get to school or work on time. Plenty of other people here are tourists, slowly meandering through the plaza and taking in the atmosphere. Carlos looks up at his father, who is smiling. He is happy to be home again.

RINGING IN THE NEW YEAR

Every New Year's Eve, thousands of Spaniards crowd into Puerta del Sol, while millions more watch the festivities live on television or online. At midnight, the clock on the Real Casa de Correos, a government building in the plaza, chimes twelve times. With each chime, celebrants pop a grape into their mouths. They believe that eating these twelve grapes will bring them good luck in the coming year.

A PALACE AND A MASTERPIECE

Javier steers the boys through winding streets to find their hotel and drop off their bags. Back outside, Javier asks if they are ready to see the city, and Leo blurts out, "I'm hungry." Carlos rolls his eyes—Leo is always hungry. Javier laughs and tells them he knows just the place for breakfast. He leads them to Chocolatería San Ginés, a famous restaurant that has been in operation since 1894. Its specialty is churros, long fried doughnuts. Spaniards often buy them from street vendors and eat them as their morning meal or later as a snack. The churros come with cups filled with sweet, thick hot chocolate for dipping.

Chocolatería San Ginés is one of Madrid's oldest chocolate shops.

Once they are satisfied, the three travelers set out on foot for their first stop. In planning their first day in Spain, Javier decided that each of them would pick a different destination. His choice is the Palacio Real, or the Royal Palace, which he had loved touring as a child. While they walk to the palace, Carlos asks if they will get to see Felipe VI, the current king of Spain. His dad says they probably will not. Although the Palacio Real is the king's official residence, he actually lives in a more modest palace just outside Madrid. Most of the Palacio is now used as government office space, although some of its almost 3,000 rooms are open to the public.[1]

At the Palacio Real, a tour guide leads them through room after room filled with elaborate furnishings and chandeliers. Its walls are covered with beautiful tapestries and paintings. In the ornate Throne Room, the ceiling is painted with images of Roman gods. The guide explains that construction on the palace began in the early 1700s under the reign of King Felipe V. He wanted a grand palace because he was jealous of his French cousins' luxurious palace at Versailles. Felipe's palace originally was supposed to have some 12,000 rooms, but the project was scaled down after his death.[2]

Their next destination is Carlos's choice. He loves to draw and has been learning more about painting in art class. When he told his art teacher that he was going to Spain, she lent him a book about paintings by Spanish artists. His favorite paintings from the book are displayed at the Museo Nacional Centro de Arte Reina Sofía. Popularly known as the Reina Sofía, this art

THE GOLDEN TRIANGLE OF ART

The Reina Sofía and two other nearby museums in Madrid—the Museo del Prado and the Museo Thyssen-Bornemisza—are known as the Golden Triangle of Art. The Museo del Prado is one of the most renowned art museums in the world. Its collection includes a wealth of masterpieces by European painters, including the famous Spanish artists Diego Velázquez and Francisco Goya. The Museo Thyssen-Bornemisza showcases what was once the private art collection of Baron Hans Heinrich Thyssen-Bornemisza, who died in 2002. The museum's nearly 1,000 paintings include works by leading artists from the 1200s to the 1900s.[3]

museum has a collection of 22,000 works of modern art from around the world.[4]

As they walk through the galleries, Carlos excitedly points out paintings from the book. He is most eager to see *Guernica* by Spanish painter Pablo Picasso. His art teacher told him that Picasso is considered one of the most important and influential artists of the 1900s, and many art experts think *Guernica* is his greatest masterpiece.

Measuring about 11.5 by 25.5 feet (3.5 by 7.8 m), *Guernica* is so large that the museum dedicated a whole room to it.[5] When the family gets there, the room is filled with visitors, but slowly they make their way to the front of the crowd. Leo had seemed bored as they toured the galleries, but even he is awed by the painting's power, letting out a loud "wow" as he looks at it. Carlos tries to understand the painting's chaotic scene rendered in shades of black, gray,

Visitors at the Museo Nacional Centro de Arte Reina Sofía can order something to eat or drink at its restaurant NuBel.

and white. He can make out a mutilated corpse, a wounded horse, and two women wailing in pain and grief. One of them holds the body of her dead child.

After they leave the museum, Javier explains the painting to Carlos and Leo. It depicts the 1937 aerial bombing of a town in northern Spain. At the time, Spain was in the middle of the Spanish Civil War (1936–1939), during which General Francisco Franco led troops who wanted to make him dictator. Franco was behind the bombing, which killed more than 1,600 people and left the town in ruins.[6] When Carlos asks who won the war, Javier responds that Franco did. For nearly four decades, Spain suffered as Franco ruled with an iron fist.

THE TEMPLO DE DEBOD

Not far from the eastern end of Gran Vía stands one of Spain's most unexpected landmarks, the Templo de Debod. Construction on the temple began in the 100s BCE in the ancient city of Meroë in the kingdom of Kush, also called Cush, located in what is now Sudan. In the 1900s, Egypt gave the temple as a gift to Spain in appreciation for the country's generous donations to preserve other ancient structures. The temple was dismantled, shipped to Madrid, and rebuilt stone by stone before being opened to the public in 1972.

BIG LUNCH, BIG GAME

After a brief Metro ride, they arrive at Gran Vía, Madrid's major commercial street. By now, it is three o'clock in the afternoon. It's time for *la comida*, the heartiest meal of the day in Spain. About 1,000 stores, restaurants, and theaters line the wide road, many on the ground floor of elegant milky-white buildings that were built on Gran Vía

during the early 1900s.[7] Knowing it will annoy his dad, Leo mischievously points out a McDonald's in one of those stately structures. Javier shakes his head and reminds them of his rule: When you are in Spain, you will eat like a Spaniard.

Javier leads them down a side street and finds the restaurant he has been looking for. He tells them that it has been run by the same family for decades and that he had often eaten there as a child. Outside, they stop before a chalkboard with the menu, which lists low-cost three-course specials available that day.

Javier, Carlos, and Leo start their meal with gazpacho, a cold tomato soup with chunks of vegetables. For their main courses, Javier insists they each get something different so they can sample one another's dishes. Carlos orders paella, a dish made of rice colored yellow by a spice called saffron and mixed with meats, seafood, and vegetables. Leo gets *cochinillo asado*, or roasted suckling pig, and Javier orders *merluza al horno*, or roasted hake. Carlos loves the paella and pork, but he is uncertain about Javier's fish dish. After one bite, though, its delicious tomato-flavored sauce makes him wish he had ordered it.

As they finish their feast with a dessert course of flan, a sweet baked custard, Leo is ready to start his activity. His choice is no surprise. As the best soccer player in his school, Leo wants to go to the Santiago Bernabéu Stadium, the home stadium of Real Madrid, the city's most beloved *fútbol* team. Fútbol is Spanish for "soccer."

They arrive at the stadium early enough to take a tour before the game. The tour includes a museum with exhibits about the team and its players. It also has a model of the newly renovated

Santiago Bernabéu Stadium was named after a former legendary Real Madrid president.

stadium, which has a seating capacity of more than 80,000 and a retractable roof.[8] Leo especially enjoys the Trophy Room, with its rows of golden cups won by Real Madrid.

At first, Carlos isn't too interested in the soccer match. But as Javier and Leo, who are both big Real Madrid fans, point out favorite players and shout at great plays, Carlos gets caught up in the excitement. When the game ends with victory for Real Madrid against FC Barcelona, Real Madrid's biggest rival, he cheers along with everyone else in the crowd.

Madrid is home to about 3.3 million people, while around 1.7 million people live in Barcelona.[10]

The sun has just set when they get back to Puerta del Sol, but at night, the plaza is even busier than it had been that morning. As they pass a fountain, Javier tells the boys that many Spaniards love staying out late, having fun in the streets and public plazas. They stop a moment to join a crowd listening to a street musician playing classical songs on the guitar. Then they head to a nearby restaurant for a light dinner of *jamón* (ham), *Manchego* cheese, and bread.

As they eat, Javier outlines the plan for the rest of their vacation. After two more days in Madrid, they will head north to Barcelona, Spain's second-largest city. It is known for its beautiful architecture, exciting nightlife, and tasty Catalan food. By taking a high-speed train, they can make the 313-mile (504 km) trip in just under three hours.[9] After a few days there, they will stop off in the city of Zaragoza to visit Javier's childhood friend. Then the family will return to Madrid and fly home.

Javier pauses for a moment and looks upset. Carlos asks if there is anything wrong. His dad replies that a week in Spain just does not seem enough. He wants to show the twins so much more. Carlos has an idea. The three of them could come back again next year. His dad says they will have to see, but from Javier's smile, Carlos feels confident they will be revisiting Spain soon.

THE MANY SIGHTS OF SPAIN

Carlos learned what many first-time travelers to Spain quickly discover. There are far more exciting things to see and do in Spain than anyone could possibly experience in one brief trip. The country is full of natural beauty, with fields of colorful flowers, great groves of olive trees, wetlands full of birds and other wildlife, and snowy peaks that reach high into the air. The hills of the mountainous north are a hiker's delight, while the nation's winding network of roads provides cyclists with an ideal way to tour the country's varied terrain. For beachgoers, the pristine sands of the resorts on Spain's islands and along the Mediterranean coast are perfect places to laze away warm summer days and nights.

Spain also offers visitors a captivating countryside, home to quaint towns still committed to traditional ways. There, residents celebrate local festivals similarly to how their ancestors did centuries before. The Roman ruins and medieval castles that dot the landscape offer visual evidence of the country's rich history.

The country's cities, on the other hand, are filled with busy streets, crowded buses and subways, and tall high-rise apartments and office buildings. These highly urbanized settings

The Pyrenees is a mountain range that divides Spain and France.

show how Spain has become a prosperous, modern nation in recent decades. In large cities, many Spaniards and tourists enjoy a vivid street culture and nonstop nightlife, where restaurants and dance clubs are open late.

Spanish cities also boast many world-class museums. They offer perhaps the best representation of Spain, with their celebration of the old and the new. Historic paintings hang alongside new works by emerging artists. Many Spaniards respect and revere their past while they keep an eager eye toward the future.

CHAPTER **TWO**

GEOGRAPHY

Spain is located on the far southwestern tip of Europe. It is just southwest of France and north of the African country of Morocco. With a land area of 192,657 square miles (498,980 sq km), Spain is the third-largest country in western Europe. It is about twice the size of the US state of Oregon.[1]

The nation sits on the Iberian Peninsula, covering about 85 percent of that landmass.[2] With a coastline stretching 3,084 miles (4,964 km), most of Spain borders bodies of water.[3] The Atlantic Ocean and the Bay of Biscay line Spain's northern border. Meanwhile, the Mediterranean Sea sits southeast of the country. Directly to Spain's south is the Strait of Gibraltar. The Gulf of Cádiz borders the nation's southwestern region.

Spain also has 1,214 miles (1,953 km) of land borders. It shares its longest land boundary with

Las Teresitas beach is almost one mile (1.6 km) long on the largest Canary island, Tenerife.

MAP OF SPAIN

KEY:
- Capital
- City
- Point of Interest

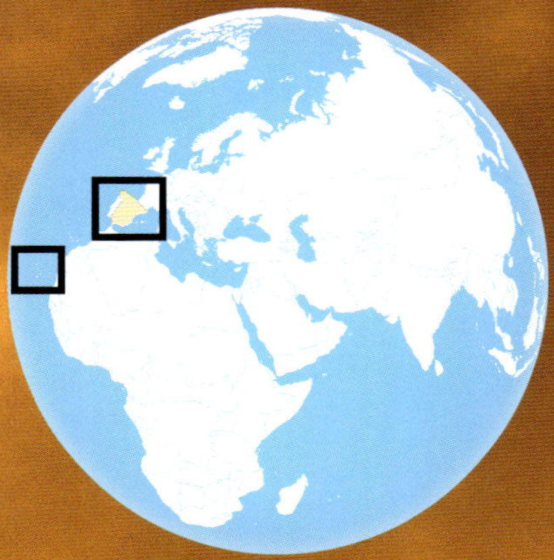

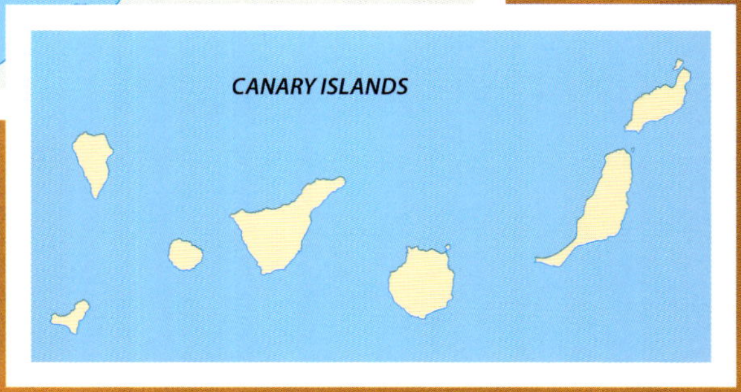

Portugal, the nation that occupies most of the western edge of the Iberian Peninsula. The border between Spain and Portugal spans 761 miles (1,224 km). Spain's second-longest land border is with its northern neighbor, France. This border extends 401 miles (646 km) but is interrupted by a 39-mile (63 km) land border with the tiny country of Andorra.[4] The small nation is sandwiched between Spain and France.

Spain also shares a 0.7-mile (1.2 km) land border with the United Kingdom along Gibraltar, a small enclave located on a peninsula on Spain's southern coast.[5] Gibraltar was controlled by Spain until 1713. In that year, the country ceded the territory to Great Britain, later known as the United Kingdom, in the Treaty of Utrecht.

THE ENCHANTED CITY

Ciudad Encantada is known worldwide for its strange and spectacular rock formations. Located in the village of Valdecabras, Ciudad Encantada is also called the Enchanted City. Wind, water, and ice eroded the limestone rocks over centuries. People visiting the Enchanted City marvel over how some of the naturally formed rocks resemble carvings of ships, animals, and human faces.

OFF THE MAINLAND

Spain also controls several small areas of land off the Iberian Peninsula. The Spanish port city of Melilla is located on a peninsula along the northern coast of Morocco. It was conquered by Spain in 1497. Spain also holds Ceuta, a city on the Moroccan coast near the entrance of the Strait of Gibraltar from the Mediterranean Sea. Spain took control of Ceuta in 1580, and this was formalized by the

A famous tram runs along Majorca's western coast.

terms of the 1668 Treaty of Lisbon with Portugal. Melilla and Ceuta are parts of Spanish North Africa, which also includes the islands of Peñón de Vélez de la Gomera, Peñón de Alhucemas, and Islas Chafarinas.

The Balearic Islands, located east of the Spanish mainland in the Mediterranean Sea, are also part of Spain. The archipelago includes five major islands in addition to many smaller ones. The largest islands in the chain are Majorca, Minorca, Ibiza, Formentera, and Cabrera. While Majorca has a mountain range and Ibiza features rolling hills, Minorca is largely flat. All boast beautiful beaches that draw many tourists every year.

Spain's Canary Islands are found in the Atlantic Ocean off the northwestern coast of Africa. The island chain was created millions of years ago by volcanic eruptions. The largest islands in the group include Tenerife,

Fuerteventura, and Gran Canaria. The Canaries feature an extremely diverse landscape of mountains, volcanoes, tropical forests, sandy coves, and desert dunes. The peak of Pico de Teide on Tenerife stands at 12,198 feet (3,718 m). It is the highest point in all of Spain.[6]

VARIED TERRAIN

Most of the Spanish mainland is part of a large, dry plateau called the Meseta. The Meseta is roughly half a mile (0.8 km) above sea level.[7] Its flatlands are dotted with large hills and low mountains. The area includes Mulhacén, mainland Spain's highest mountain, which lies in the Sierra Nevada along the Meseta's southern edge. *Sierra Nevada* literally means "snowy range." It is home to many resorts that cater to skiing enthusiasts.

Standing at 11,421 feet (3,481 m), Mulhacén's peak is the highest on the Iberian Peninsula.[9]

Mountain ranges border the Meseta to the south, east, and north. The Sierra Nevada and the Sierra Morena are found in the south. The Iberian Mountains are located east and northeast of the Meseta. North of the plateau lie the Cantabrian Mountains, where much of Spain's forested land is located.

One of the country's most impressive mountain ranges is the Pyrenees in the northeast. These mountains are found along the neck of the Iberian Peninsula at Spain's border with France. The Pyrenees stretch more than 270 miles (435 km) from the Bay of Biscay on the Atlantic Ocean to the Mediterranean Sea.[8] The largest mountains are found at the center of the range.

The Pyrenees' highest peak is Aneto in Posets-Maladeta Natural Park, rising to an elevation of 11,165 feet (3,403 m).[10]

Low-lying areas in Spain include the coastal plains along the Mediterranean Sea in the country's east and south. This area features some of Spain's richest farmland. Broad fertile plains also stretch across the Ebro Basin in the northeast and the Guadalquivir Basin in the southwest. Despite the Guadalquivir Basin's high temperatures, irrigation helps farmers there cultivate citrus orchards.

Flowing through these basins are two of Spain's major rivers, the Ebro and the Guadalquivir. The Tagus is another important Spanish river. Flowing 626 miles (1,007 km), the Tagus is the country's longest river.[11] It flows from the Meseta into Portugal and empties into the Atlantic Ocean. The Guadalquivir, Douro, and Guadiana Rivers similarly flow into the Atlantic. Among Spain's prominent rivers, only the Ebro leads to the Mediterranean.

During the summer, most rivers in Spain have low water levels, making them difficult to navigate. Along the Spain–Portugal border, the Guadiana River's flow dramatically decreases in August and September to less than 10 percent of its year-round average.[12] Only the Ebro River has a relatively

SPAIN'S BLUE FLAG BEACHES

Blue Flag is an international program run by the Foundation for Environmental Education in Copenhagen, Denmark. It awards its Blue Flag designation to beaches, marinas, and tourism boats that maintain extremely high environmental and safety-related standards. In 2024, Spain had 639 Blue Flag beaches, more than any other country in the world.[13]

During the 2021 to 2022 season, Spain grew more than 3.6 million short tons (3.3 million metric tons) of oranges.

consistent flow. During hot months, melting snow from the northern mountains combined with summer rainfall replenishes the river.

CLIMATE AND RAINFALL

Although average temperatures vary from region to region, much of Spain has a temperate climate year-round. Its pleasant weather is one of the reasons it is a popular destination for vacationers from around the world. Unsurprisingly, the country's most comfortable weather is found in areas that most attract tourists. The warm, sun-drenched summers on the Mediterranean coast, the Canary Islands, and the Balearic Islands are especially welcoming. The Canaries

The Meseta covers more than 81,000 square miles (210,000 sq km).

BRINGING WATER TO ANDALUSIA

In Andalusia, a region in southwestern Spain, scientists are applying a 1,000-year-old solution to the problem of water shortages. During the Middle Ages, the Moors, a Muslim population that had controlled the Iberian Peninsula, built a network of channels called acequias. These channels guided melted snow from the northern mountains to Andalusia's fields. Abandoned during the 1960s, the acequias are being restored to irrigate agricultural lands threatened by repeated droughts.

have average temperatures in the winter of 64 degrees Fahrenheit (18°C) and in the summer of 76 degrees Fahrenheit (24°C).[14]

The Meseta in central Spain tends to experience hotter summers and cooler winters. In the middle of the plateau, Madrid has an average summer temperature of 77 degrees Fahrenheit (25°C) and an average winter temperature of 48 degrees Fahrenheit (9°C). Throughout the year, the Meseta is usually sunny and dry. It typically receives less than 15 inches (38 cm) of rainfall per year.[15]

Spain's southwest experiences the hottest temperatures in the country. In the summer, the temperature often rises above 104 degrees Fahrenheit (40°C). The coolest region is the north, especially in the mountains. Winds from the Atlantic Ocean bring moisture, creating cloudy and foggy conditions there. Much of the year, rain falls in a steady drizzle over the northern mountains. Heavy rainfalls can hit the region during winter, resulting in an average annual rainfall of about 39 inches (99 cm).[16] On the highest mountains, peaks are covered in deep snow.

Due to the relatively low amount of rainfall in most of Spain, the country has long experienced droughts in the summer. But in recent years, the effects of climate change have worsened the problem. Going into the spring of 2023, Spain had experienced many months of below-average rainfall. That season, the country had an extreme drought that dried up fields, destroyed crops, and depleted reservoirs.

A severe heat wave caused by a warm, dry air mass from North Africa added to the crisis. It brought summer temperatures in spring. The southern city of Córdoba was just shy of 102 degrees Fahrenheit (39°C), the highest temperature ever recorded in Spain during April.[17] With droughts and high temperatures continuing, some experts fear Spain will undergo desertification. Unless the country can find new water supplies, much of the Spanish landscape could become desert by the end of the century.

One possible solution is desalination technology. Desalination plants are facilities that remove salt from seawater, creating fresh water suitable for irrigation and human consumption. In 2024, Spain operated about 100 of these plants. The Spanish city of Torrevieja, located on the Mediterranean coast, runs the largest desalination plant in Europe. It can create more than 60 million gallons (227 million L) of fresh water a day.[18] But desalination can be costly. Some people think that the technology will improve and become cheaper. Others worry that the large amounts of energy used in the desalination process could worsen the emissions that cause climate change.

With many desalination plants, Spain is the biggest user of desalination in Europe.

CHAPTER **THREE**

PLANTS AND ANIMALS

Fields turn bright red as springtime poppies bloom. Agile Pyrenean chamois easily climb rugged mountainsides and cliffs. Flamingos add a shock of pink to the scenery as they feed in the wetlands. And a Spanish imperial eagle swoops through the air above massive snowy peaks.

Spain offers many spectacular encounters with flora and fauna. It is one of the most biologically diverse countries in Europe. Many of Spain's species are endemic, meaning they can be found only in that country. Endemic species are particularly prevalent in Spain's mountainous regions and on its islands. Forty-four percent of the animal species living on the Canary Islands are endemic.[1]

Many Pyrenean chamois live in the Pyrenees mountains.

La Palma is one of the Canary Islands. Known for its trees, La Palma is called the Green Island.

PLANT LIFE

Spain is home to about 8,000 species of plants.[2] Before humans, most of the land that is now Spain was covered with forests. The only areas naturally inhospitable to tree growth are high up in the mountains, in the southeast's extremely dry areas, and on the Canary Islands. However, forests were cleared to make way for farms, pasturelands, and urban areas. Since the 1940s, the Spanish government has tried to combat deforestation. But these plans have often been met with resistance, especially in areas where farmers want to preserve grazing lands for sheep, goats, and other livestock.

Forests now cover about 37 million acres (15 million ha), or about 30 percent of the country.[3] Dense woodlands are largely confined to the northern mountainous regions. The trees that thrive in this area include oak, beech, and pine. Drought-resistant palm trees and pine species grow in hot, dry areas in the south. Other trees found in Spain include chestnut, elm, poplar, hazelnut, maple, and eucalyptus.

Grasslands also span large swaths of Spain. Esparto grass is historically important to Spain. Common in the southeast, this grass was traditionally used for making products such as paper, rope, and baskets. In the spring and summer, many plants bloom throughout Spain. Red poppies, gold broom, purple lavender, and yellow sunflowers fill the countryside with color. In the Balearic Islands, Majorca is home to one of Spain's earliest blooms. During January, bright white flowers sprout in almond groves, giving the appearance of a blanket of snow covering the warm island.

THE EUCALYPTUS THREAT

The eucalyptus tree, native to Australia, was introduced to Spain in the 1800s. During the 1950s, the Spanish government promoted the establishment of eucalyptus plantations in the northwestern community of Galicia. People used the eucalyptus trees to make paper products. Soon these fast-growing trees replaced native trees in the region. Eucalyptuses pose a major problem for Galicia. As more wildfires sweep the area, the highly flammable eucalyptuses make the fires especially destructive.

ANIMALS IN THE WILD

Spain is home to between 50,000 and 60,000 species of animals.[4] They include a wide range of mammals. The Spanish ibex is found only on the Iberian Peninsula. It is also called the Iberian ibex. This species of mountain goat's big hooves and short legs allow it to easily cross rocky mountainsides. Also endemic to Spain is the Iberian lynx. This rare lynx is identified by the beard of fur around its face, black tufts at the top of its ears, and spotted coat.

While the lynx is a large cat, many small cats also inhabit the country. The spotted genet is usually seen only in Africa, but some live in southwestern Spain. A distinctive black stripe runs down its forehead. It also has black patches under its eyes.

Among Spain's most impressive mammals is the brown bear, which roams the country's northeastern forests. These large bears have big paws, strong jaws, thick coats, and the ability to stand on their hind legs. Other mammals found in Spain include wild boars, deer, wolves, squirrels, rabbits, badgers, foxes, and pigs.

Many birds of prey fly over Spain, including the bearded vulture, peregrine falcon, eagle owl, and goshawk. The most revered is the Spanish imperial eagle, which is the country's national bird. These large birds have a wingspan of more than six feet (1.8 m).[5] Other bird species native to Spain include flamingos, herons, geese, storks, spoonbills, and bustards. Spain also serves as a stopover for many birds as they migrate between Africa and Europe.

Many bird-watchers flock to Tablas de Daimiel National Park in the region of La Mancha.

ISLANDS OF DOGS?

Many people assume the Canary Islands were named after the canary, a small bird native to the islands. But the bird was actually named after the islands, not the other way around. The name *Canary* comes from the Latin name *Canariae Insulae,* meaning "islands of the dogs." The ancient Roman writer Pliny the Elder reported that the islands were inhabited by a "multitude of dogs of a huge size." A modern theory proposes that the animals the writer saw were not dogs but monk seals. These animals were once prevalent on the islands but are now nearly extinct.

Spanish imperial eagles can weigh 5.5 to 10.6 pounds (2.5 to 4.8 kg).

Observing from elevated wooden walkways, visitors can spot more than 200 species of birds in the park.[6] This wetland area is filled with plant and animal life.

Spain has designated about 300 nature reserves, 152 natural parks, 30 natural spaces, and 17 geoparks.[7]

Wetlands are also habitats for Spain's population of amphibians and reptiles. These animals include many species of lizards, snakes, geckos, turtles, frogs, and toads. Numerous types of insects are native to Spain as well, such

Bottlenose dolphins are the largest dolphin along Spain's coasts.

as bees, ants, crickets, grasshoppers, and butterflies. At times, desert locusts come to southern Spain from North Africa.

With its long coastlines and many islands, Spain has a rich assortment of marine life, including mackerels, tuna, octopuses, swordfish, and anchovies. The diversity of fish and shellfish is especially notable off the southern coast, where the waters of the Atlantic Ocean and the Mediterranean Sea meet. In the south, dolphins and whales can be seen near the Strait of Gibraltar. Bottlenose dolphins are also found off the Ebro River delta on the Mediterranean coast. The inlets and caves along the Mediterranean are home to monk seals. Long hunted for their fur, meat, and oil, the population of Mediterranean monk seals has been reduced to only a few hundred animals. They are an endangered species.

PROTECTING SPAIN'S WILDLIFE

Dozens of species of Spanish wildlife are at risk of extinction. Overhunting is one reason for this. Another factor is climate change, which has led to rising temperatures and an increased risk of wildfires that can destroy plant and animal habitats. The growth of Spanish tourism is also accelerating human encroachment on previously wild spaces and endangering wildlife there.

Some of the endangered species include animals that are symbols for Spain, including the Spanish imperial eagle and the Iberian lynx. However, conservationists have made dramatic improvement in protecting Iberian lynx. In 2000, the large cats were on the list of critically endangered species, with only approximately 100 individuals left in Spain. In 2024, the lynx population had grown to more than 2,000.[8] The species was no longer considered endangered and was upgraded to the vulnerable list.

SAVING HER SPECIES

An Iberian lynx named Aura played a vital role in the continuing survival of her species. When she was born in 2002 in Doñana National Park, there were only 94 lynx there. A conservation group selected her to help grow the Iberian lynx population. Over her life, she gave birth to 14 kittens, and they went on to have their own kittens. By the time of her death in 2022, Aura was the ancestor of more than 900 Iberian lynx.[9] She helped save her species from extinction.

In Spain, Iberian lynx live in and around Doñana National Park and in the Sierra Morena mountain range.

The Spanish government has long worked to preserve the country's natural environment. In 1916, King Alfonso XIII established the country's national park system. After the creation of Sierra de las Nieves National Park in Andalusia in 2021, Spain became home to 16 national parks.[10] Among these wild spaces is Teide National Park on the island of Tenerife. With four million visitors annually, it is the most popular national park in Europe.[11] By protecting these natural spaces, Spain hopes to ensure that the country's rich plant and animal life will thrive for generations to come.

CHAPTER **FOUR**

HISTORY

Stone tools found at various archaeological sites suggest that humans occupied the area that is now Spain as early as 1.2 million years ago. Paintings of animals in the Altamira cave in northern Spain are thought to have been created between 24,000 and 10,000 BCE. By about 3200 BCE, people now referred to as Iberians had developed a distinct culture. They lived in large villages and raised crops and livestock. The Iberians made pottery and tools, and they crafted objects from copper.

EVOLVING CULTURE

In the 1000s BCE, Phoenicians from the eastern shores of the Mediterranean Sea arrived in Spain. They traded with the Iberians and established settlements on Spain's eastern and southern coasts. About 100 years

At 8.2 feet (2.5 m) long, a doe is the largest figure on the Altamira cave's ceiling.

later, the first Celtic people landed in the north. Greeks arrived by about 600 BCE and created trading posts along the eastern coastline. Iberian culture evolved to reflect the impact of all these groups. Phoenicians and Greeks brought with them new goods such as glass and ivory. The Celts taught the Iberians metalworking skills that allowed them to make iron tools and ornaments.

People from the North African coastal city of Carthage came to Spain in the 400s BCE. They had built a successful trading system along the Mediterranean. Carthage went on to conquer much of the Iberian Peninsula, which includes the lands that are now Spain and Portugal, by the 200s BCE.

In 218 BCE, the famous Carthaginian general Hannibal led soldiers from Spain into present-day Italy to attack the Romans. This set off the Second Punic War (218–201 BCE). After Hannibal's defeat in 203 BCE, Spain was invaded by Romans. Over the course of about 200 years, the Iberian Peninsula became fully integrated into the mighty Roman Empire. The Romans called the area Hispania. This is what the country's Spanish name, España, is derived from.

Under Roman rule, infrastructure was built in Spain, including hard-surface roads and aqueducts that transported water to dry regions. The Romans updated Spanish cities. They also spoke Latin, which in Spain developed over time into the modern Spanish language. The Romans introduced Christianity. It became the official religion of Spain around 380 CE, when Spain was still part of the Roman Empire.

Germanic tribes, including the Visigoths, started moving into Spain during the 400s CE, quickening the collapse of the Roman Empire. During that era the Visigoths and the Spanish population clashed. However, the Visigoths were still able to establish a monarchy that ruled the

Iberian Peninsula. The Visigoths' centralized government was weakened due to infighting among rival nobles. These conflicts grew far more heated as King Roderick took the throne in 710. Enemies of the new monarch asked for help from Tāriq ibn Ziyād, the governor of Tangier in North Africa, to remove Roderick from power.

Tāriq's armies were successful. They took over Spain in 711 and quickly conquered the Iberian Peninsula. Known as the Moors, this civilization would go on to dominate the country for about seven centuries.

Under the Moors, Spain was greatly influenced by advanced Islamic culture. Brilliant mathematicians, physicians, writers, and philosophers introduced a wealth of new ideas. Cities also prospered under the Moors, who constructed great palaces and mosques, Islamic houses of worship. Their distinct architecture featured great arches and domes, geometric

In May 711, Tāriq ibn Ziyād led 7,000 soldiers to overtake Spain.

designs, beautiful ornamentation, and intricate tile work. The Spanish language was also transformed as Muslims introduced Arabic words into Spanish.

THE UNIFICATION OF SPAIN

The Moors' hold on the Iberian Peninsula was threatened by Christian kingdoms in northern Spain. The kingdom of Castile was a particularly powerful force during the Reconquista, the Christian movement to expel the Moors from the area beginning in the early 800s. By about 1250, the Reconquista conquered enough territory that the Moors were confined to the small kingdom of Granada in Spain's far south. With the exception of Granada and the small Christian kingdoms of Aragon and Navarre, Castile controlled most of Spain.

In 1469, Prince Ferdinand of Aragon and Princess Isabella of Castile married. They ruled both kingdoms after they rose to their respective thrones. After these monarchs took hold of Granada in 1492 and seized Navarre in 1512, they ruled the entirety of modern Spain.

Ferdinand and Isabella wanted Spain to be a Christian state. But people with other beliefs lived there. The rulers encouraged hatred of Muslims and Jews. They started the Spanish Inquisition, a

AVERROËS

Abū al-Walīd Muhammad ibn Ahmad ibn Muhammad ibn Rushd was born in 1126 in Córdoba, which is now Spain. Better known by the names Averroës or Ibn Rushd, the Muslim philosopher integrated Islamic beliefs and Greek thought. He wrote about Aristotle's and Plato's works and their impact on Muslims and Europeans. Many people read Averroës's work to better understand philosophy, and he continues to shape the field.

period in which people who were not Christian were jailed or killed. Thousands of Spaniards fled the country so they would not be persecuted for their religion. Not everyone was able to leave. Some converted to Christianity. Others pretended to be Christian but continued their devotion to their own religion in secret.

EL CID'S LEGACY

El Cid has a complicated history in Spain. The nobleman served as a soldier during the Reconquista era. Many Spaniards considered him a hero, a belief heightened by an epic poem written about him in the late 1100s and early 1200s. However, recent historians have challenged the legend of El Cid. They explain that the real El Cid, Rodrigo Díaz de Vivar, was an opportunistic mercenary, willing to fight for whatever side would pay him more.

EXPANDING TO THE AMERICAS

In 1492, Isabella and Ferdinand helped fund an expedition headed by Italian explorer Christopher Columbus. He planned to sail west to find a new sea route to India and China. Columbus instead arrived at several islands in the Caribbean. This prompted a race among European nations to explore the Americas and claim land, despite Indigenous peoples already living there.

The Spanish monarchy sponsored many more expeditions, including ones led by Juan Ponce de León, Vasco Núñez de Balboa, Hernando de Soto, and Francisco Vázquez de Coronado. Many explorers used violence to dominate the Native populations they encountered. Hernán Cortés led the killing of thousands of Aztec people, who lived in what is now Mexico. Francisco Pizarro committed acts of genocide against the Incas of present-day Peru.

MINI **BIO**

DIEGO VELÁZQUEZ

In the early 1600s, Spain became an important cultural center in Europe. A leading figure in this arts movement was painter Diego Velázquez. Born in Seville in 1599, Velázquez later traveled to Madrid in search of fame and fortune. He soon became a painter for the royal court and was close to King Philip IV. The king often visited Velázquez's studio to watch him paint.

Most of Velázquez's paintings depicted the royal family and their friends. His most famous painting, *Las Meninas*, shows Velázquez painting a portrait of the king and queen while maids and court jesters attend to the young princess Margarita Teresa. Because of its composition and innovative use of light and color, *Las Meninas* is considered one of the greatest paintings of all time.

In 1658, Philip IV made Velázquez a knight. The artist held ceremonial roles in the royal court. He died in 1660 and is still considered one of Spain's most important cultural figures. Many of Velázquez's paintings are displayed at the Prado Museum in Madrid.

Diego Velázquez was an influential Spanish artist of the 1600s. Some consider him to be a giant in Western art.

By exploiting the people and riches of the Americas, Spain amassed great wealth. It also took control of vast swaths of land in North and South America and expanded its reach into Europe and North Africa. With its wealth, land holdings, and strong army and navy, Spain was one of the most powerful countries in the world in the 1500s.

AN EMPIRE IN DECLINE

In 1588, Spain was dealt a blow when its mighty fleet of ships, known as the Spanish Armada, was defeated by the English navy. Spain was battling England to bring it under Spain's control but lost. Weak rulers and religious wars also hastened the empire's steady decline throughout the 1600s. Spain lost control of most of its American and European colonies in the 1700s.

By the early 1800s, Spain's lands outside the Iberian Peninsula included small enclaves in North Africa and the islands of Cuba, Puerto Rico, Guam, and the Philippines. Spain was forced to surrender most of these holdings after its defeat in the Spanish-American War (1898). Cuba became an independent nation, and the United States took possession of Puerto Rico, Guam, and the Philippines.

The weakened Spain also experienced turmoil at home. Spanish citizens were dissatisfied with the monarchy, the Catholic Church, and an ailing economy. They also didn't have much political power. These factors led to a revolt in 1873. Spain's First Republic period began after King Amadeus abdicated the throne that year. But the new government struggled to lead. Spain's army challenged the new government and restored the monarchy in 1874.

Alfonso XIII was king of Spain from 1902 to 1931.

Much of the world experienced turmoil as World War I (1914–1918) broke out. Spain remained neutral, and its economy was bolstered by exports to fighting nations. But after the war, the Spanish public increasingly expressed anger against the government. The people were upset with high unemployment rates and government corruption.

To suppress criticism, King Alfonso XIII helped install General Miguel Primo de Rivera as a dictator. Growing political tensions forced de Rivera to resign in 1930, and King Alfonso allowed free elections. The elected leaders told the king to abdicate. After he refused, he was forced to leave the country in 1931.

During the Second Republic, elected officials approved a new constitution that established Spain as a democratic republic. Catholicism would no longer be the country's national religion. The Catholic Church's political power decreased, and Spain's government gained more control. Some hoped that Spain would experience more freedom of religion.

The new government supported labor unions, higher wages for workers, and increased political control for the country's regions. But political infighting continued. Left-wing supporters of the republic included union workers and socialists. Their right-wing opponents were dominated by the military, church officials, and defenders of the monarchy.

THE FRANCO ERA

In February 1936, a new election brought the Popular Front, an alliance of left-wing groups, into power. Many in the military were upset with the election outcome. Weeks later, General Francisco Franco and army officers talked about overthrowing the Popular Front. In July, members of the military stationed in Morocco rebelled against the new government. Soon military members on mainland Spain followed. Franco led the rebellion.

By September, the Spanish Civil War (1936–1939) had begun. Supporters of Franco and the rebels were known as Nationalists. Supporters of the Spanish republic were called Republicans. While most countries, including the United States, officially remained neutral, the Nationalists received support from Italy and Nazi Germany. The Republicans found allies in Mexico and the Union of Soviet Socialist Republics (USSR).

More than 350,000 Spaniards died in the Spanish Civil War.[1]

In 1939, the Nationalists won the conflict, and Franco was established as the leader of an authoritarian government. The government used violence and intimidation to maintain its control. Anyone perceived as an enemy of the regime risked being imprisoned or killed. Franco widely restricted personal freedoms and used censorship to reduce public criticism. Many Spanish writers, artists, and intellectuals fled the country.

Democracies around the world shunned Franco and his regime for its human rights abuses. In response, in the 1940s and 1950s, Franco pursued economic policies to make Spain self-sufficient, including taxing foreign goods and promoting government ownership of industries. But Franco's policies led to more poverty and suffering for the Spanish people.

By the late 1950s, the country's economy was close to collapse. Franco's regime enacted reforms to make the economy function like those of Spain's prosperous neighbors in western Europe. It also sought foreign investment and worked to build its tourism industry. The result was a period of rapid economic growth nicknamed *El Milagro Español*, or "the Spanish miracle." The economy was further bolstered by more than one million Spanish laborers who moved to other European countries, such as Switzerland and West Germany.[2] These workers sent money home to help their struggling families.

MODERNIZING SPAIN

Franco named Prince Juan Carlos, the grandson of King Alfonso XIII, as his successor. The dictator died in 1975, ending his control over the country. After being sworn in as king, Juan Carlos set about making sweeping political and social reforms. In June 1977, Spain held its first democratic elections in 40 years. The legislature immediately began drafting a new constitution, which resembled the one instituted in 1931. With its adoption, Spain became a constitutional monarchy. The new government repealed all laws of the Franco regime and guaranteed democratic freedoms to its citizens.

Spain wanted to join an alliance of nations called the European Economic Community, which would later become known as the European Union (EU). Before gaining admission in 1986, the Spanish government had to stabilize its economy. The country also embraced the international community by hosting high-profile events. Barcelona was home to the 1992 Summer Olympics. That same year, Seville presented the Expo '92 world's fair. By embracing other nations, Spain's economy improved. As with many countries, Spain was rocked by an economic downturn that began in 2008. By early 2020, Spain's economy had benefited from five years of growth and job creation. However, at the beginning of the COVID-19 pandemic, the Spanish economy dramatically shrank. Soon the country began to recover, which was partially due to tourism.

REMEMBERING THE FRANCO ERA

In 2007, Spain passed a law meant to help citizens come to terms with the Spanish Civil War and its aftermath. The law called for the removal of all monuments dedicated to dictator Francisco Franco. It also allowed families of people killed by Franco's troops to exhume their loved ones from mass graves for reburial. Some people didn't want to disturb the burial sites. But Prime Minister José Luis Rodríguez Zapatero, whose grandfather died during the conflict, countered that Spain needed to acknowledge what had happened to heal as a nation.

SEPARATIST GROUPS

While Spain experienced violence after its 1936 election, the nation largely succeeded in nonviolently transforming its government after Franco's death in 1975. Spain traded its authoritarian dictatorship for a modern republic. But the country still had conflict. In 1981, the military threatened to overtake the government. Juan Carlos spoke to the nation and restored order.

Spain has several separatist groups that seek political independence. Among these groups are the Basques, who have sought to form their own nation. The Basques are a cultural group concentrated in an area in northern Spain and southern France known as Basque Country. They have lived in that region for thousands of years.

The vast majority of Basque people are peaceful. But a small faction of extremists called the Euskadi Ta Askatasuna (ETA) was founded in 1959. This terrorist group has used bombings and assassinations to pressure the Spanish government to grant Basque independence. This included an assassination attempt on King Juan Carlos in 1995. Because of its violent tactics, the ETA has almost no support among Basques. After years of negotiating a ceasefire, the ETA finally surrendered its

Some call Tolosa, Spain, the cultural heart of Basque Country.

Prime Minister Pedro Sánchez negotiated the amnesty law for Catalan separatists.

stockpile of weapons in 2017. The next year, the organization announced that it was ending all political activities.

Some people in Catalonia, a region in far northeastern Spain, have also campaigned for political independence. In 2017, Catalan separatists planned a vote on a referendum calling for independence. A Spanish court found that the referendum violated the Spanish constitution and banned the vote, but the separatist government decided to hold the election.

Spanish police arrived to shut down the election. They used force to try to prevent people from voting, which injured some voters, and Spain ended the Catalan government. Law enforcement arrested hundreds of people involved in holding the vote, charging them with misuse of public funds and civil disobedience. Nine separatist leaders were jailed for sedition, which means inciting a rebellion against the government. After years in jail, they were pardoned by the Spanish government in 2021.

In May 2024, Spain's legislature passed a law granting those arrested amnesty, thus dismissing their legal cases. Prime Minister Pedro Sánchez supported the measure, in part because he needed to maintain an alliance with the Together for Catalonia political party to stay in power. But he presented the law as a way of putting the conflict behind them so all Spaniards could peacefully coexist. Since 2017, the momentum behind the Catalan separatist movement has slowed, but it remains to be seen whether the group will resume its push for an independent state.

CHAPTER **FIVE**

PEOPLE AND CULTURE

Spain is home to approximately 47 million people.[1] Ethnically, its population is fairly homogeneous. Most Spaniards can trace their ancestry from groups who arrived on the Iberian Peninsula during ancient and medieval times. The groups include Phoenicians, Greeks, Carthaginians, Romans, Germanic peoples, Celts, and Arabs.

Since Spain's geography made travel within its borders difficult for most of its history, some regionally based groups have developed strong cultural identities. Members of these groups consider themselves as part of a separate nation. These groups include the Catalans in the northeast, the Basques in the north-central

About 85 percent of Spaniards have Spanish ancestry.

region, and the Galicians in the northwest. The most notable cultural differences between these peoples are the languages they speak.

MANY TONGUES

As established by the constitution of Spain, the country's official language is Castilian Spanish. About 75 percent of Spain's population speaks this language.[2] This type of Spanish is derived from Latin, the language of the ancient Romans.

Castilian emerged as dialect in northern Spain. The kingdoms of Castile and Leon spoke the language. When Spain was unified in the 1400s, Castilian became the country's dominant language. Today, Castilian accents and vocabulary vary slightly within different regions of the country.

Catalan is the official language of Catalonia and the Balearic Islands. It is spoken by about 17 percent of Spain's population.[3] Catalan is derived from Latin and closely related to Occitan, a language spoken in southern France.

The province of Valencia speaks Valencian. The question of whether Valencian is a dialect of Catalan

THE GITANOS

Spain's southern region of Andalusia is the traditional home of the Gitanos, one of Spain's largest ethnic groups. They are a subset of the Roma people. Today, several hundred thousand Gitanos live in Andalusian cities as well as Madrid and Barcelona. Some Gitanos continue to lead a traditional nomadic way of life, while others have assimilated into the larger Spanish society. The Gitanos have experienced a lot of discrimination and prejudice. But they have stood up against the injustices they faced. In 1986, the Gitanos formed the Union of the Gitano People, a political organization that advocates for their rights.

THE SAGRADA FAMÍLIA

One of the most famous landmarks of Barcelona is the Sagrada Família, a grand Roman Catholic church designed by Spanish architect Antoni Gaudí. He began work on the ambitious project in 1882. After 1910, he devoted all his time to its construction and even moved into his workshop on the site. When Gaudí died in 1926, his masterwork was still incomplete, but building continued. In 2024, officials said the Sagrada Família was estimated to be finished in 2026. When it is finally completed, its high-spindled towers will make it the tallest church in the world.

or a separate language is a political issue. Another language spoken in Spain is Galician, which is closely related to Portuguese. Most Galicians are bilingual in Galician and Castilian.

The Basques' language is Euskara, though it is sometimes called Basque. Its origins are unclear, although Euskara is known to predate the Roman Empire's control over Spain. Spoken by about 2 percent of Spain's population, Euskara is not related to any other language used today.[4] Arabic is often spoken in Spanish North Africa, but it is not an official language there.

ARCHITECTURE, ART, AND MUSIC

Throughout Spain, one of the country's most prominent and enduring cultural achievements is its architecture. In the countryside, ruins of ancient buildings are everyday reminders of Spain's past as part of the Roman Empire. Hundreds of castles and

The royal library is one of the thousands of rooms inside the Monastery of El Escorial.

palaces date back to the early days of united Spain. One of them is the Monastery of El Escorial. The complex has more than 4,000 rooms and was built in the late 1500s.[5] It also holds the tombs of Spanish monarchs.

Vast churches and cathedrals, such as the grand Gothic cathedral in Seville, show the impact the Catholic Church had on Spain. In the south, many churches were once mosques dating to the era of the Moors. The most famous site in Granada is the Alhambra, whose ornate carvings and rounded arches make it an excellent example of Moorish architecture. Spanish cities are also full of modern marvels. Barcelona is especially known for its unusual buildings designed by Antoni Gaudí, who was one of the most influential architects of the 1900s.

Spain has also produced many world-renowned visual artists. During Spain's Golden Age in the 1500s and 1600s, leading painters included El Greco and Diego Velázquez. In the early 1800s, Francisco Goya produced passionate, often political works, including his famous *The Third of May*

1808 painting. Salvador Dalí and Joan Miró were hailed for their experiments in surrealism, but the most famous Spanish artist of the 1900s was Pablo Picasso. His works included paintings, sculptures, drawings, graphics, and ceramics. The work of these artists can be found in many museums throughout Spain.

Folk songs and dances are popular in every region of Spain. Among the most beloved are the flamenco music and dance of the Gitanos, Spain's Roma ethnic minority. Developed in Andalusia in southern Spain, flamenco songs tell tragic tales of romance. The accompanying dance involves intricate footwork, hand clapping, and finger snapping. Considered a uniquely Spanish art form, flamenco dancing is still performed in nightclubs in many cities.

Flamenco dancers often move to the strumming of a guitar.

One of Spain's greatest gifts to the world may be its popularization of the guitar. In the 700s, the Moors brought a stringed instrument called the oud to Spain. The oud led to the creation of the modern guitar. In Spain, the guitar emerged as a primary instrument of folk music performed by the Gitanos.

LITERATURE AND FILM

Spain has a long and storied tradition of literature. One of the most famous Spanish novels is *Don Quixote* by Miguel de Cervantes, which was published in the early 1600s. The book tells the story of an aging man who, deluded by tales of romance and chivalry, styles himself as a knight. Considered the first modern novel, *Don Quixote* is one of the most widely translated books in the world.

Among Spain's most famous writers is dramatist and poet Federico García Lorca. Born in 1898 in Spain's Granada province, Lorca drew upon the folklore of the Gitanos of Andalusia in much of his writing. His notable works include the poetry collection *Roma Ballads* and the tragic play *Blood Wedding*.

Franco's Nationalist forces targeted Lorca for his socialist views and his homosexuality, arresting Lorca in 1936. Socialism advocates that resources and property are collectively owned and equally shared within a society. Lorca was not given a trial and was executed by Nationalist forces in 1936. Lorca has since been celebrated not only for his contributions to literature but also as a heroic fighter against the forces of fascism. Other Spanish writers of the 1900s include poet Vicente Aleixandre and novelist Camilo José Cela, both of whom won the Nobel Prize for Literature.

Although Spain's film industry is small, it has produced several internationally recognized directors. Filmmaker Luis Buñuel was born in Calanda, Spain. He spent much of the Franco era in

MINI **BIO**

PENÉLOPE CRUZ

Penélope Cruz is the first Spanish actress to win an Academy Award. Born in 1974, she grew up outside of Madrid. For nine years, she studied classical ballet at Spain's National Conservatory before making her film debut in *Jamón, Jamón* in 1992. The same year, she received international attention for the critically acclaimed film *Belle Epoque*.

In 1997, she began her long creative relationship with Spanish filmmaker Pedro Almodóvar. Cruz soon also started acting in Hollywood films, including *Vanilla Sky*. She won an Academy Award for her supporting performance in *Vicki Cristina Barcelona*. In 2010, Cruz married her costar in that film, Spanish actor Javier Bardem.

In Hollywood, Cruz proved herself adept in different genres by appearing in the musical *Nine*, the action blockbuster *Pirates of the Caribbean: On Stranger Tides*, and the broad comedy *Zoolander 2*. Among her latest successes in the Spanish film industry was her 2021 Academy Award–nominated performance in *Parallel Mothers*. Her seventh film directed by Almodóvar, it tells the story of two single mothers dealing with the lasting legacy of the Spanish Civil War.

Penélope Cruz gained success on the Spanish screen to become an international star.

exile, but he returned to his native land in the 1960s to make *Viridiana*. The film tells the story of a young nun. The Catholic Church found the movie's use of religious imagery offensive and labeled it blasphemous. Franco banned the movie. Buñuel went on to win acclaim for films such as *Belle de Jour* and *The Discreet Charm of the Bourgeoisie*.

More recently, Pedro Almodóvar has inspired a loyal following of moviegoers with his satirical comedy-dramas. His works include the 1988 film *Women on the Verge of a Nervous Breakdown* and a 1999 movie called *All About My Mother*. The Spanish film industry also launched the careers of performers such as Academy Award–winning actors Penélope Cruz and Javier Bardem.

SPANISH CUISINE

Spaniards are also proud of their contributions to world cuisine. Like in other Mediterranean countries, cooks in Spain make liberal use of olive oil, garlic, and fresh vegetables. Commonly used spices include cumin, paprika, tarragon, and saffron. The country's most popular meats are pork, chicken, and beef. For holidays and other occasions, many celebrate with lamb. Spain also consumes a lot of seafood. The waters off the country's coastlines provide it with a bounty that includes crabs, squid, sardines, tuna, and codfish. Legumes are also a staple of the Spanish diet, with lentils and chickpeas being especially popular.

Different regions in Spain are famous for certain dishes. Catalonia is known for its fish casseroles and cured meats. Galicia offers diners plenty of seafood, including baby eels and codfish. Gazpacho is popular throughout Spain. Tomatoes, garlic, and cucumbers make this cold

Many Spaniards enjoy a cold bowl of gazpacho during the hot summer.

soup, which originated in Andalusia. Paella—saffron-flavored rice mixed with seafood, meats, and vegetables—is a nationally recognized dish, but traditionally it was associated with Valencia. Known for raising cattle, the Castile region boasts flavorful roasts.

Spain is also known for its tapas. These small plates are commonly served in bars, where Spaniards meet family and friends before lunch or dinner for a snack and a drink. There are hundreds of different tapas, but common ones include marinated seafood, mushrooms in garlic sauce, and omelets. Adults often drink wine with meals, sometimes in the form of sangria, a mixture of wine and fresh fruit. Other popular beverages are mineral water, beer, soft drinks, and strong black coffee.

SPORTS AND BULLFIGHTING

By far the most popular sport in Spain is soccer. At many large stadiums, soccer matches are held on Saturdays and Sundays between August and May. The nation's most famous teams are Real Madrid and FC Barcelona. Soccer fans across Spain celebrated when the Spanish team won the World Cup in 2010. Another exciting victory was winning the Union of European Football Associations championship in 2012. The Spanish team that claimed the title is now considered among the greatest national teams in the history of soccer.

At the 1984 Olympics, Spain won the silver medal in basketball. The team's win helped popularize the sport throughout the country. Many Spanish sports fans also follow tennis and cycling. One of the country's greatest sports heroes is cyclist Miguel Induráin, who won the Tour de France five consecutive years in the 1990s.[6]

Bullfighting is one of the sports most associated with Spain. Dating from the Middle Ages, bullfights remain popular spectacles throughout the country. Most cities have a bullring, but the most famous one is Las Ventas in Madrid.

THE BULLFIGHTING CONTROVERSY

In 2013, the Spanish government officially declared that bullfighting was a vital part of the country's cultural heritage. But bullfighting is extremely controversial within Spain. For many years, animal rights activists have condemned the spectacle, insisting that torturing and killing an animal for entertainment is immoral. Bullfighting has also become a political issue, with conservative politicians generally supporting it and liberal politicians generally opposing it. A 2019 poll found the Spanish public was divided on the question, with 25 percent of respondents in favor of bullfighting, 56 percent opposed, and 19 percent indifferent on the issue.[7]

Historians do not know the exact origin of bullfighting.

Many Spaniards celebrate St. Patrick's Day. The holiday comes from Christianity.

Approximately 2.3 million people watched Spanish bullfights during the 2018 to 2019 season.[8] The bullfighting season starts in late March and ends in early October.

Many fans consider bullfighting more of an art form than a sport. Bullfighters, known as matadors, are praised for their grace and courage as they face down bulls one-on-one, waving their capes to draw the animals closer. The life-and-death struggle between the matador and bull is dangerous for both. But bullfights usually end with the matador stabbing the bull to death. Many animal rights activists have raised concerns about this tradition and question whether the entertainment is worth bulls being killed.

A CATHOLIC NATION

Throughout much of Spain's history, Roman Catholicism has been a strong force in its culture and society. It was the country's official religion until the constitution of 1978 was adopted. According to that document, Spain has no national religion, and people of all faiths within its borders have the freedom to practice their religion. The constitutional right to religious freedom was a direct response to abuses during the Franco dictatorship, which had severely restricted the rights of people who were not Catholic.

While the majority of Spaniards are still Roman Catholic, a growing number of people are atheists or don't participate in any religion. A small percentage of the population belongs to other Christian denominations. Many people also practice other religions, such as Islam, Judaism, Buddhism, and Hinduism.

Even with the reduced influence of Christianity in Spain, many of the country's public holidays still have ties to the religion. One celebration is All Saints' Day, which takes place on November 1. Many Spaniards, even those who are not Christian, exchange gifts for Three Kings' Day on January 6.

About 58 percent of Spaniards practice Roman Catholicism.[9]

The Spanish calendar also observes some nonreligious national holidays. May 1 is Labor Day, while December 6 marks the adoption of the nation's constitution. The liveliest secular holiday is National Day, which is observed on October 12 and commemorates explorer Christopher Columbus's arrival in the Americas. On National Day, people come out for parades, sporting events, and performances designed to celebrate Spain and its people. Spaniards come together on this day to celebrate their culture.

CHAPTER **SIX**

POLITICS

Every December 6, schools and businesses close so the people of Spain can celebrate Constitution Day. With parties and parades, they commemorate an important moment in the country's history. On December 6, 1978, Spanish voters approved a new constitution. Spain's flag is often featured at these celebrations.

The 1978 vote marked a crucial step in Spain's transformation from a dictatorship to a democracy. Constitution Day is a reminder that the national government is still very young by western European standards. It also allows Spaniards to reaffirm the ideals set out in their government's founding document, including a commitment to freedom, justice, and equality.

Spain's Congress of Deputies held a ceremony to celebrate Constitution Day in 2022.

THE MONARCH AND OTHER SYMBOLS OF SPAIN

The constitution establishes Spain as a parliamentary constitutional monarchy, with the monarch as the head of state. Felipe VI began serving in that role in 2014, when his father, King Juan Carlos, abdicated the throne. The monarch performs some important functions, such as ratifying laws, declaring war, and signing treaties negotiated with other nations. However, the monarch is not a politician and is supposed to remain neutral. This person also serves as a symbol of national unity, presiding over ceremonies and attending diplomatic meetings.

In addition to the symbolic function of the monarchy, Spain also formally recognizes three national symbols in the 1978 constitution and its subsequent laws. One is the Spanish national flag, which features red and yellow stripes.

The use of these colored stripes originated during the reign of Carlos III in the late 1700s. At the time, white flags were flown on many warships. The king wanted to create a new naval flag that would make Spanish warships easier to identify. Out of twelve candidates, he chose two that incorporated red and yellow stripes.

A KING'S SPEECH

In modern Spain, the role of the monarch is largely ceremonial. But in 1981, King Juan Carlos was instrumental in saving Spain's democratically elected government. A group of military officers tried to take over the government in a coup. Early in the morning, the king went on television to declare his faith in democracy and demand the coup leaders stand down. After his speech, the rebellion collapsed, and its leaders were taken into custody. One Spanish politician said, "This proves the value of having a king."[1]

On the left side of the national flag appears another official symbol of Spain—the Spanish coat of arms. At its center is a shield, divided into quarters and topped by a royal crown. In each quarter is a symbol of one of the traditional kingdoms of Spain: Castile, Leon, Navarre, and Aragon. At the shield's bottom is an image of a pomegranate representing Granada. Two columns appear on each side. They represent the Pillars of Hercules, which the ancient Greek hero was said to have placed at Gibraltar and Ceuta. Red ribbons winding around the pillars bear the motto *Plus Ultra,* which means "Further Beyond." The saying alludes to the far-flung colonies once controlled by the Spanish Empire.

Spain's third national symbol is its national anthem, "Marcha Real." The song is traditionally known as the "March of the Grenadiers" or the "Royal March." The military song has no words, making it one of four national anthems without lyrics. The composer of this song is unknown. At first, the tune was not formally designated as the

HEIR TO THE THRONE

Recent financial scandals have damaged the Spanish royal family's reputation. These conflicts have led some Spaniards to question whether they need a monarchy at all. The person making the strongest case for the monarchy might be Princess Leonor of Asturias, King Felipe's eldest child and next in line for the throne. Popular with the Spanish public, the princess swore an oath to the constitution during a nationally televised ceremony in 2023. Held just after she had turned 18, this ceremony signaled her readiness and willingness to serve as the nation's queen.

national anthem. But the Spanish public knew the song since it was customarily played at events attended by the monarch.

A 1997 law made two versions of the anthem official. One was the entirety of the song and the other was a shortened version. The law also designated when each version was to be played. The long version is played for the monarch, while the short version is for the prime minister. The shorter version is also used at sporting events and informal occasions. At official events, the anthem must always be played in its entirety without interruption.

THE EXECUTIVE AND LEGISLATIVE BRANCHES

Spain's prime minister is the head of government. This official manages the government's day-to-day operation. The monarch proposes a new prime minister after an election for Spain's national legislature. The nominee is usually the leader of the political party with the majority of legislators. The lower house of the legislature then votes on the monarch's nomination.

Sometimes no political party has a majority, so parties will join to form a coalition government from which the prime minister is chosen. This scenario played out in 2020 when Pedro Sánchez was named prime minister for the second time. He first held the post in 2018.

The prime minister appoints a cabinet, which is called the Council of Ministers. Each minister oversees a particular area of the national government. For example, Spain's ministries include defense, health, culture, and more. The prime minister may select one or more deputy prime ministers. Deputy prime ministers can step in for the prime minister if the prime minister cannot

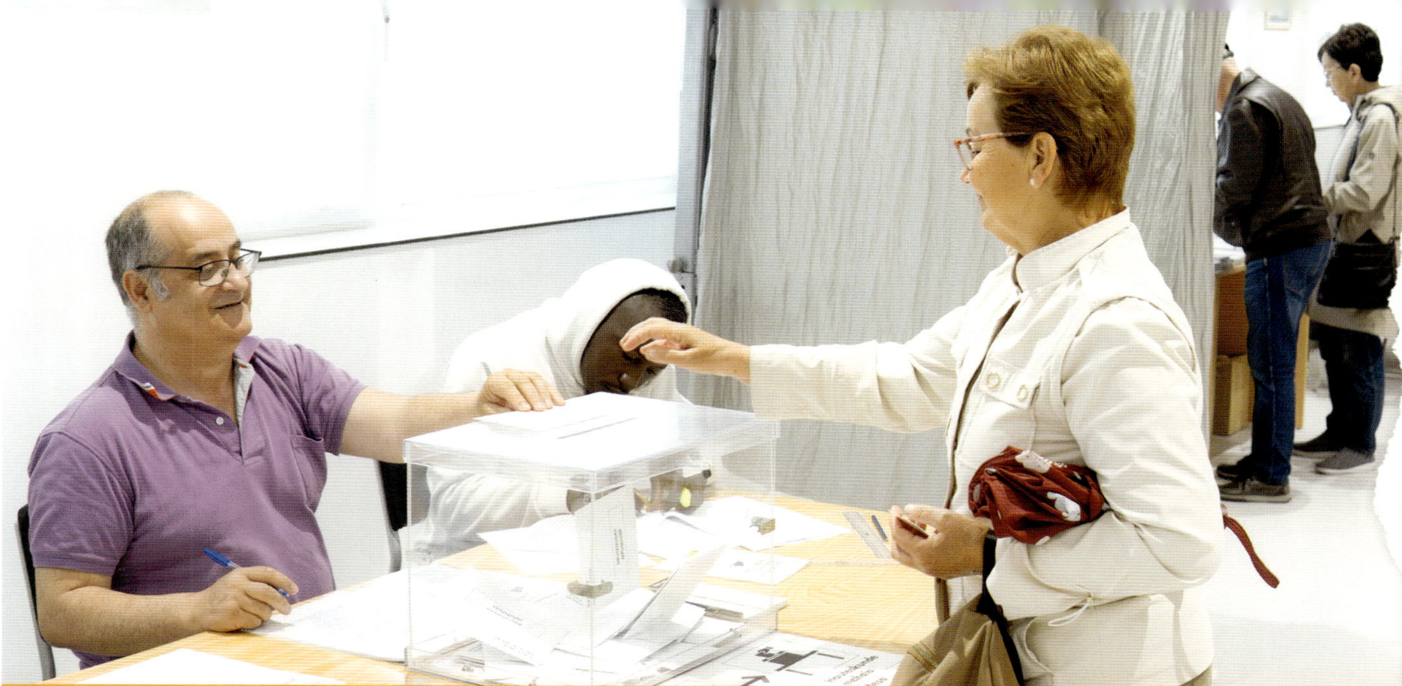

Spanish women gained the right to vote in 1931.

do the job. They can head government departments. The executive branch of the government also includes the Council of State. This council makes recommendations about policies, but the government is not required to adopt its proposals.

The Cortes Generales is Spain's national lawmaking body. It is composed of two houses, the Congress of Deputies with 350 seats and the Senate with 265 seats. The Congress of Deputies generally has more power than the Senate. Both houses have often had more female members than many national legislatures in the world. Women usually make up about one-third of the Congress of the Deputies and about one-fourth of the Senate.[2] Women make up about half of Spain's population.

Members of both houses serve four-year terms. The legislatures of regional governments appoint 57 of the senators. The remaining 208 senators and all the deputies are elected by citizens. Spaniards 18 years or older are allowed to vote. People who are born in Spain do not automatically receive citizenship. Instead, citizenship is conferred only to people with at least one parent who is a Spanish citizen. Political parties decide what candidates will appear on ballots instead of individual candidates filling out forms to be on the ballot.

During Franco's dictatorship, Spain had only one political party, the Falange. Soon after his death, the Cortes voted to legalize the formation of other political parties. By 1977, Spain had 156 political parties. Over time, various alliances between these different groups have developed and dissolved. Since the early 1980s, power has mostly shifted between two large parties, the left-wing Spanish Socialist Worker's Party and the center-right Popular Party.

AN ELECTION SURPRISE

One of the most dramatic elections in modern Spain occurred in the spring of 2004. The right-wing Popular Party was in power and expected to win. But, on March 11, three days before the election, the country was rocked by terrorist train bombings that killed 191 and injured more than 1,800 people.[3] The Popular Party blamed the Euskadi Ta Askatasuna (ETA) for the attacks, but news came out that it was a different terrorist group. Many Spaniards became furious with the Popular Party. In a surprise victory, the rival left-wing party won the March 14 election, propelling its relatively unknown leader, José Luis Rodríguez Zapatero, to be prime minister.

Other major parties include the Basque Nationalist Party and the Galician Nationalist Bloc. A national far-right party called Vox has emerged in recent years. In 2018, it became the first right-wing party to win seats in the Cortes since Franco's death in 1975.

REGIONAL AND LOCAL GOVERNMENTS

According to the constitution, the national government must share power with regional governments known as autonomous communities. Spain is divided into 17 autonomous communities, which function similarly to US states. Each autonomous community's government has a president and a legislature. The government also recognizes two autonomous cities, Ceuta and Melilla, located along the coast of Morocco.

The national government has control over matters such as defense and foreign policy. But autonomous communities do have substantial control over some aspects of their regional government, such as education and culture. Because the powers that belong to the central government and the powers that belong to the autonomous communities are not precisely defined, the national government has often come into conflict with regional governments. Some communities, such as Catalonia and Andalusia, have long pushed for more control over their affairs. As a result, the powers held by regional governments vary widely.

Below Spain's national and regional governments, the nation has provincial and municipal levels of local government. The country is divided into 50 provinces, which are each governed by a provincial council. Autonomous regions that have their own province do not have

There are 50 provinces and 8,117 municipalities in Spain.[4]

provincial councils. The council members, who are elected by citizens, choose the mayor.

Municipal governments pass local laws and sometimes levy taxes, although they also receive funds from the national and regional governments. Provincial governments monitor municipalities to ensure they are cooperating with one another. They can also provide services that small municipalities cannot afford.

THE JUDICIARY AND THE MILITARY

Spain's judicial system establishes courts at each level of government. The highest national court in Spain is the Supreme Court. The monarch appoints Supreme Court justices from candidates provided by the General Council of the Judiciary. This council is the governing body of the entire judicial system. It includes 20 judges and lawyers who are appointed to the council for five-year terms.

Similar to the Supreme Court, the Constitutional Court also has jurisdiction over all of Spain. But the Constitutional Court judges only whether laws violate the constitution and settles disputes between the national government and autonomous communities. The National High Court is assigned cases dealing with terrorism, drug trafficking, and offenses against the monarch or government officials. Each autonomous community has a High Court of Justice with four divisions: criminal, civil, employment, and judicial review. Provincial courts hear both criminal

The High Court of Justice of Andalusia is the highest court in that autonomous community.

and civil cases. Lower courts include courts of first instance, courts of judicial proceedings, penal courts, and municipal courts.

The Spanish military is composed of an army, navy, and air force. In the past, adult men were required to serve for nine months, but since 2002 military service has been voluntary.[5] The Spanish National Police and the Civil Guard are charged with maintaining security within Spain's borders. Established in 2006, the Emergency Response Unit coordinates disaster relief.

CHAPTER **SEVEN**

ECONOMICS

In the early 1900s, the Spanish economy was struggling. Many Spaniards lived in poverty in the largely agricultural nation. At the same time, other countries of Europe, such as Germany, France, and the United Kingdom, had thriving industries and growing economies. During the 1950s and 1960s, the Spanish government acknowledged the need for modernization to compete in the world economy.

Spain's economic changes allowed it to become part of the eurozone, the set of countries in the EU that share the common currency of the euro. The alliance also helped stabilize Spain's economy when it was struggling in 2012. By the 2020s, these changes helped transform Spain into one of the most economically successful countries in Europe.

Tourism is an important sector of the Spanish economy. Benidorm is a top tourist destination in Spain's Costa Blanca region.

During the 2022 to 2023 season, Spain produced 1.6 million short tons (1.5 million metric tons) of olive oil.

AGRICULTURE AND FISHING

In the 1950s, about half of all Spaniards worked in the agricultural, forestry, and fishing industries.[1] Today, these sectors employ only a small percentage of workers. However, modern farming techniques now allow Spain to better utilize its farmlands and pastures. Irrigation has transformed areas with dry soil into productive fields.

Spain's agricultural sector leads the world in the production of lettuce and sunflower seeds. The country is also a major grower of fruits such as peaches, pears, strawberries, and tangerines. Other crops include barley, wheat, corn, rice, onions, potatoes, and tomatoes. Fields in the south and east grow an abundance of grapes. As a result, Spain is the third-largest producer of wine after France and Italy. Great groves of olive trees occupy the Andalusia region of southern Spain. These trees allow the country to manufacture about one-third of the world's supply of olive oil.[2]

Pastures cover about 16 percent of Spain.[3] This land is used to raise a variety of farm animals, including beef and dairy cattle, chickens, goats, and pigs. Sheep are also important domestic animals because they can thrive in Spain's arid conditions. About half of the country's agricultural income comes from animal products.[4] Famous for its serrano ham, the nation is a leading exporter of pork. Its meat industry also produces poultry, beef, and lamb. Other products derived from livestock include eggs, milk, raw wool, and leather.

Spain imports more timber than it produces. But its small forestry industry utilizes its pine, poplar, oak, and eucalyptus forests. In Spain's southwest, the cork oak supplies the nation with its most important forestry product. Spain is one of the largest producers of cork in the world.

For centuries, fishing has been a significant industry in Spain, especially along its northern coast. Today, that coast has the largest fishing

HIGH UNEMPLOYMENT

In 2023, the Spanish government celebrated when the country's unemployment rate fell to 11.6 percent, the lowest rate in 15 years. But another statistic dampened enthusiasm among economists. Spain's jobless rate was still almost double the average rate of countries in the EU.[5] The reason for Spain's persistently high unemployment rates is unclear. One theory blames Spain's dependence on tourism and construction, seasonal industries that leave workers vulnerable to job loss in the offseason. Another theory suggests that too many companies in Spain are small businesses without the money to invest in more workers.

fleet in Europe. Fishers' catches often include yellowfin tuna, sardines, mackerel, and pollock. Canned seafood products made in Spain include cod, tuna, sardines, squid, anchovies, and octopus. Increasingly, the fishing industry is making use of aquaculture, or commercially raising fish and other types of seafood. Spain's biggest aquaculture product is mussels. In 2023, Spain was the world's third-largest mussel producer, behind Chile and China.[6]

MINING AND MANUFACTURING

In ancient times, seafaring Phoenicians arrived in Spain, eager to make use of the land's rich array of minerals. Their interest in its mineral wealth may have given the country its name. In Spain, the nation is called España, which may have been derived from Phoenician words meaning "place where metals are forged."

Taking advantage of modern exploration techniques, miners still extract many minerals in Spain. They include iron ore, lead, zinc, potash, and copper. The geographic region known as the Iberian Pyrite Belt, which stretches into Portugal, contains one of the world's biggest sulfide deposits.

Spain once had substantial deposits of coal in the Cantabrian Mountains, but they have largely been depleted. The country has only small reserves of natural gas and oil. Spain has had to import these fossil fuels to meet its energy needs, although increasingly the country is developing its renewable energy industries. About half of its electricity now comes from hydroelectric, wind, and solar power.[7]

The Cantabrian Mountains stretch about 180 miles (300 km) along Spain's northern coast.

Since the 1950s, Spain has dramatically built up its industrial sector, which employs about 20 percent of its workforce.[8] One of its largest industries is automaking, with companies such as Ford, Renault, and the Spanish firm SEAT manufacturing vehicles there. An important and long-standing industrial area, Barcelona is home to factories that produce chemicals, metal

Spain's construction industry grew in the early 2020s, fueled by large construction projects across the country.

products, processed foods, textiles, and clothing. The city of Bilbao is known for its production of iron and steel, while Valencia is a center for the manufacturing of paper, clothing, and footwear. Madrid is also an important industrial hub, with transportation networks that reach into Africa, North America, and the rest of Europe.

In recent years, many Spanish companies have lent engineering and construction expertise to the building of large public works projects, such as dams, highways, and high-speed trains. The government has also made large investments in science and technology. These investments have helped grow the biotech, electronics, renewable energy, and telecommunications industries in Spain.

In the early 1900s, Spain imported most of the industrial products it needed. By the early 2000s, however, it became a major exporter of manufactured goods. Among its chief exports are automobiles, machinery, and electrical equipment. Other products exported from Spain include fruits, vegetables, iron, steel, chemicals, clothing, and shoes. From other countries, Spain imports crude oil, natural gas, vehicle parts, and food products. Its two largest trading partners are France and Germany, but Spain also does significant trade with China, Italy, Portugal, the Netherlands, the United Kingdom, and the United States.

THE SOL DE MIRÓ

Since 1984, Turespaña, the government agency charged with promoting Spanish tourism, has been using a logo called the Sol de Miró. This abstract image of the sun was created by famed Spanish artist Joan Miró. According to Turespaña, the colors of the logo symbolize what Spain has to offer visitors from around the world: black for "our character, strong and intense," yellow for the "light and joy of our sun," red for "our passion," and green for "our landscapes full of nature."[11]

THE SERVICE SECTOR

In terms of employment, the service sector is the largest part of the Spanish economy. About 75 percent of workers provide services rather than create goods for sale.[9] Service industries include education, banking, retail sales, communications, consumer services, government services, and other professional work, such as practicing law and medicine.

In Spain, many service workers—such as restaurant employees, hotel workers, and tour guides—are part of the tourism industry. In fact, the jobs of approximately 10 percent of all Spanish workers are related to tourism. Each year, approximately 55 million tourists visit Spain, making it a major vacation destination.[10] Most tourists in Spain are from other European countries, such as France, Germany, Italy, the United Kingdom, and the Netherlands. They come for Spain's sunny, temperate climate and its many attractions, including museums, historic buildings, festivals, and beautiful scenery. But the greatest draws for many tourists are Spain's pristine beaches and the luxurious resorts that dot its southern coastline.

As record numbers of vacationers travel to Spain each year, some Spaniards have begun to speak out against the tourism industry. They complain that tourist areas are overcrowded and that the outsiders are disrupting local cultures. With apartments and houses being occupied by travelers, the cost of rent is being driven up for Spanish citizens. In recent years, there have been protests against tourism on island resorts and across the mainland. At one dramatic demonstration in Barcelona in the summer of 2024, crowds of protesters chanted "tourists go home" while spraying tourists with toy water guns.[12]

Spain has 363 airports, 93,274 miles (150,110 km) of roads, and 9,624 miles (15,489 km) of railroad tracks.[13]

TRANSPORTATION IN SPAIN

The Spanish government has invested heavily in its transportation system, making it easier to enter Spain and travel within its borders. Its vast road system was overhauled in the early 2000s to ease congestion and decrease traffic jams. Starting in the 1990s, the government also devoted resources to its train network. The first high-speed train route from Madrid to Seville was opened in time for the

KILOMETER ZERO

A stone slab in the pavement of Puerta del Sol, a city plaza in Madrid, marks Kilometer Zero. The spot is often considered the geographical center of Spain, but it isn't the exact center. Kilometer Zero is also the starting point of six national roads, which stretch beyond Madrid and connect the capital to other major urban centers. Distances on these roads are measured by how far they are from the Kilometer Zero plaque.

Expo '92 world's fair. In 2008, another route began transporting passengers from Madrid to Barcelona. A regional train ride between these two cities takes almost nine hours, while the high-speed train takes only two hours and 45 minutes.[14]

Because of its lengthy coastline, Spain relies heavily on transportation through sea routes, especially for international trade. Most of the goods imported to and exported from Spain pass through the nation's ports. The most important port cities in Spain include Algeciras, Barcelona, Bilbao, and Valencia.

As the largest airline in Spain, Iberia operates both domestic routes and flights to cities in Europe, Africa, North America, and South America. Madrid's Barajas Airport is one of the busiest in Europe. Barcelona and Málaga also have large airports. Smaller international airports service foreign travelers going to vacation hot spots, including the beautiful islands of La Palma and Tenerife.

CHAPTER **EIGHT**

SPAIN TODAY

Young adults in Spain today likely lead a very different life than their grandparents did when they were young. These grandparents probably lived in a rural area and worked in agriculture. They were probably poor, with housing lacking modern conveniences such as electricity and indoor plumbing. Much of their lives were likely centered on the Catholic church they regularly attended in their village or town.

Now the typical Spanish young adult studies or works in a city. Many have service industry jobs and live in modern apartment buildings. Most rarely go to church, if they attend at all. And they usually have more money, higher levels of education, and far better health care than their grandparents did at their age.

Four-fifths of all Spaniards now live in cities.[1] The combined populations of the greater metropolitan

Barcelona features a mix of historic and modern buildings.

areas of two Spanish cities, Madrid and Barcelona, are well above five million.[2] With the growth of cities and increased travel abroad, many Spaniards have adopted new customs unknown to earlier generations. At the same time, some traditional ways and beliefs, particularly those involving Catholicism and regional cultures, are losing their hold on many modern Spaniards.

FAMILY LIFE

Traditionally, Spaniards had large families. Most city dwellers, however, tend to have fewer children. Families now have about two kids on average.[3] As in the past, though, people in Spain tend to remain close to their family members throughout their lives. Much of their social life revolves around family get-togethers, and often several generations live in the same house. It is not uncommon for young people to live in their parents' home until they get married.

Even if they are no longer churchgoers, many Spaniards still mark life milestones through Catholic

RATÓN PÉREZ

In 1894, the future king Alfonso XIII was eight years old and lost his first tooth. His mother, Queen Maria Cristina, asked royal adviser Luis Coloma to write her son a story. Drawing on folk tales, Coloma wrote about a little mouse named Ratón Pérez, who lived in a sweets shop near the Royal Palace. The mouse visited Alfonso and other children as they slept and left behind little gifts for their lost teeth. Ratón Pérez has since become Spain's version of the tooth fairy, and the shop in which he supposedly lived is a museum dedicated to this beloved character.

religious ceremonies. Babies get baptized, older children receive their first Communion, and adults wed in the church. Each of these events provides an opportunity for families to host lavish gatherings with their friends and relatives.

Despite the wide acceptance of these observances, many Spanish Catholics no longer adhere to the church's traditional stances on family life, such as prohibitions on abortion, divorce, and same-sex marriage. All of these are now legal in Spain. During Franco's dictatorship, it was often thought that women were supposed to serve men. Many people worked to secure more rights for women. Spain is now considered to be a leader in gender equality.

ORGANIZING THE DAY

In both urban and rural Spain, many people organize their days in a way that's unique in western Europe. By tradition, Spanish offices and stores open at about 9:30 a.m. and close for the day by about 8:00 p.m. During the afternoon, between about 1:30 p.m. and 4:30 p.m., these establishments close for a few hours.[4] This allows workers to return home and indulge in a long, leisurely lunch, perhaps followed by a nap, called a siesta. In late afternoon, they then return to work until closing time.

Small businesses often still adhere to these working hours, but many businesses no longer shut down during the afternoon. For instance, large shopping centers, supermarkets, and department stores now stay open during the day. Long lunch hours are also no longer convenient for many workers because they live far from where they work.

Tapas are small plates that can be eaten as appetizers or combined for a meal.

Spaniards' eating habits, however, still conform to these traditional hours. They generally begin the day with a small breakfast, often consisting of a sweet roll or toast with jam and a cup of strong coffee. Children often eat fried doughnutlike churros with hot chocolate or cold cereal with fruit.

Regardless of their working hours, Spaniards still enjoy a long lunch, the main meal of the day. Sometimes eaten over a few hours, a typical lunch includes several courses and might feature soup followed by a fish or chicken dish and end with a dessert and coffee. Dinner is a light meal usually eaten between 9:00 p.m. and 10:00 p.m., although sometimes it is served as late as midnight.

Spaniards also often snack during the day. At about 5:00 p.m., they may have a slice of bread topped by ham or a piece of chocolate. Before lunch or dinner, they may stop at a bar and meet friends for drinks accompanied by tapas. Prior to the evening meal, many people also take a brief paseo, a relaxing walk around the neighborhood.

EDUCATION AND HEALTH CARE

Spain boasts a 98 percent literacy rate.[5] From ages six to 16, all young people are required to attend school. After graduating primary school and secondary school, students between 16 and 18 can attend vocational or college preparatory classes.

Most students go to public schools, but about one-third attend private institutions, most of which are operated by the Catholic Church.[6] Since the 1980s, Catholic schools have been under the national government's supervision. They receive subsidies from the government that allow students to attend them tuition-free. Some regional governments have gained control over aspects of their education systems. For instance, in Catalonia, Galicia, and the Basque Country, students must study the languages associated with those regions.

Before the 1960s, relatively few students went to college. Now more than two-thirds of Spaniards of college age attend college or university.[7] In 2024, Spain had 89 institutions of higher learning, about 50 of which were publicly run.[8] The most prestigious include Complutense University of Madrid, the University of Barcelona, and the University of Granada. Students must pass an exam to get accepted into a university. At university, students usually devote three years to general studies and two more to a specialized area.

EL GORDO

On December 22, people all over Spain are glued to their screens, waiting to hear the winning numbers of El Gordo, a lottery operated by the Spanish government since 1812. The drawing is televised live from Madrid's opera house. During the program, local schoolchildren select the numbers and sing the results to the live audience. Winners then pop champagne and party in bars and in the streets. Most winnings are small, but those who guess all the numbers right can exchange their tickets for as much as 400,000 euros, which was equal to about $435,280 in 2024.[9]

Through the National Institute of Health, the country's government provides health care to the people of Spain. Many responsibilities for administering the health-care system fall to regional governments. Government-sponsored health care has led to great improvements in Spaniards' overall health. Their life expectancy is one of the highest in the world.

LEISURE TIME

Most workers in Spain get 25 or more days of paid vacation per year. Many take advantage of this benefit by going to beach resorts or heading to the mountains to go hiking. Even when they are not on vacation, Spaniards enjoy spending leisure time outdoors. In cities, they often spend hours relaxing with friends at sidewalk cafés or in public plazas and parks. In the countryside, they enjoy picnics as they take in the scenery. Throughout Spain, many people like to hunt and fish.

Many Spaniards spend their time off participating in sports, including soccer, cycling, and golf. Some sports are popular in specific regions. Pelota, a type of handball, is played in the Basque Country. In the mountains of Catalonia, amateur athletes go skiing and engage in other winter sports. The coast of Valencia provides great opportunities for surfing and scuba diving. Horseback riding is a favorite pastime in Asturias and Andalusia.

Spanish cities offer residents an array of entertainment options, including concerts, theater performances, and movies. Young people enjoy an active nightlife, hanging out with friends in bars and dance clubs. At home, Spaniards have access to national, regional, and foreign television programs, as well as hundreds of radio stations. Other media include about 100 daily newspapers published in Castilian as well as in regional languages.[10] The most prestigious is *El País*, a newspaper produced in Madrid, while the most widely read is *Marca*, a paper that focuses on sports. Also popular is *¡Hola!*, a magazine that features the latest gossip about celebrities. Spaniards use social media to keep in touch with friends and family. Some of the most popular services are Facebook, Instagram, and WhatsApp.

Festivals are held in cities, towns, and villages throughout the year. These celebrations often honor the Catholic patron saints believed to look after these locales, but the religious aspects of these events are usually played down. Instead, festivals are all about friends and neighbors getting together to dance and sing, attend parades and bullfights, and watch fireworks.

Some of these celebrations are famous and attract visitors from around the world. These include the Fiesta of San Fermín held every July in the city of Pamplona. For eight days, bulls run through the streets toward the local bullring. Crowds of festivalgoers run in front of the bulls, trying to move fast enough to avoid being gored by the animals' horns. Another world-renowned festival is held in Valencia on St. Joseph's Day each March. Celebrants carry *fallas,* giant wooden

LA TOMATINA

At 11:00 a.m. on the last Wednesday of August, a firework explodes in the air above the main square in Buñol, a city near Valencia in eastern Spain. Trucks then dump more than 100 short tons (90.7 metric tons) of overripe tomatoes in the square. A crowd of 20,000 people rushes in, and for one hour everyone pelts each other with the squishy fruits. This messy annual festival, called La Tomatina, has its origins in a 1945 parade, during which a rowdy crowd raided a vegetable stand and started a food fight.

Elaborate *fallas*, large sculptures of characters, decorate Valencia to commemorate Saint Joseph.

Spaniards enjoy their country's culture and look toward the nation's future.

and papier-mâché figures of comic and satirical characters. On the final day of the festival, the fallas are burned on great bonfires.

LOOKING FORWARD

For decades, Spaniards have adapted and thrived during a period of rapid change. But that era has also created several challenges the country must deal with as it moves into the future. One of the most pressing problems is a lack of affordable housing. As many Spanish people moved to urban areas in the late 1900s, not enough housing was built in cities to meet that demand. With housing prices on the rise, many lower-income families find it impossible to pay ever-increasing rents or save enough to buy their own homes.

Spaniards have a high life expectancy of 83 years. Men's life expectancy is 80.3 years, and women's is 85.8 years.[11]

Spain's growing economy has recently attracted more immigrants. Many of them are entering the country from Morocco by crossing the Strait of Gibraltar in small boats. These African immigrants often face discrimination within Spanish society. They are also exploited by employers who hire undocumented workers to perform dangerous work at low pay. But immigrants could help keep Spain's population and economy stable.

Although the country's economy has performed solidly in recent years, high rates of poverty and unemployment have diminished the living standards of many Spaniards. Young people are especially affected by this. Regional calls for independence, especially in Catalonia, still divide society and threaten the authority of Spain's national government.

In many ways, the obstacles Spain now faces seem daunting. But during its long and rich history, the nation has survived numerous challenges and struggles and emerged as one of the most vibrant nations in Europe. Given the bold resiliency of its people and their deep love of their country, Spain's finest days could very well be ahead.

ESSENTIAL **FACTS**

OFFICIAL NAME: KINGDOM OF SPAIN

GEOGRAPHY

Area: 195,124 square miles (505,370 sq km)

Highest Elevation: Pico de Teide at 12,198 feet (3,718 m)

Lowest Elevation: Atlantic Ocean at 0 feet (0 m)

PEOPLE

Population: 47.3 million (2024 est.)

Most Populous City: Madrid (3.3 million)

Ethnic Groups: Spanish, Moroccan, Romanian, other

Religions: Roman Catholicism, atheism, agnosticism, other

GOVERNMENT

Type of Government: Parliamentary constitutional monarchy

Capital: Madrid

Head of State: Monarch

Head of Government: Prime minister

Legislature: Bicameral Cortes Generales consisting of the Senate and the Congress of Deputies

ECONOMY

Currency: Euro

Major Industries: Tourism, agriculture, textiles and apparel, food and beverages, metal manufacturing, chemicals

Natural Resources: Coal, lignite, iron ore, copper, lead, zinc, uranium, tungsten, mercury, pyrite, magnesite

NATIONAL SYMBOLS

National Anthem: "Marcha Real" ("March of the Grenadiers")

National Animal: Bull

National Flower: Carnation

GLOSSARY

abdicate
To give up power or office.

archipelago
A group of islands, or a stretch of sea containing many islands.

autonomous
Free to govern oneself without the interference of a higher authority.

conservation
Purposeful, planned preservation and protection of wildlife and their habitats from exploitation or destruction.

encroachment
Movement into another being's or group's territory.

exile
A time of forced leave from a country or region.

fascism
A political system in which a person rules with unlimited power and no opposing political parties are permitted.

inquisition
A long, intense investigation.

medieval
Related to the Middle Ages (roughly from 500 to 1500 CE) in Europe.

mercenary
A soldier who fights in exchange for money.

plateau
An area of level ground that is higher than the surrounding area.

separatist
Determined to break away from a country and form an independent nation.

socialist
Describing a political and economic theory that advocates for resources and property being shared equally among members of society.

surrealism
A movement in art and literature of the 1900s that combines realistic and fantastical images.

ADDITIONAL **RESOURCES**

SELECTED BIBLIOGRAPHY

Harrison, Richard John, et al. "Spain." *Britannica*, 11 July 2024, britannica.com. Accessed 27 July 2024.

Noble, Isabella, et al. *Spain*. Lonely Planet, 2023.

"Spain." *Worldmark Encyclopedia of the Nations*. 14th ed., Gale, 2017.

FURTHER READINGS

Kohen, Elizabeth. *Spain*. Cavendish Square, 2023.

Meaney, Marian, and Belén Aguado Viguer. *Spain: The Essential Guide to Customs & Culture*. Kuperard, 2021.

Spain. DK Travel, 2024.

ONLINE RESOURCES

Booklinks
NONFICTION NETWORK
FREE! ONLINE NONFICTION RESOURCES

To learn more about Spain, please visit **abdobooklinks.com** or scan this QR code. These links are routinely monitored and updated to provide the most current information available.

MORE INFORMATION

For more information on this subject, contact or visit the following organizations:

The Hispanic Museum & Library

3741 Broadway
New York, NY 10032
hispanicsociety.org/collection

The Hispanic Museum & Library features more than 18,000 works that document the culture of Spain, Portugal, and historical Spanish colonies.

Museo Nacional del Prado

Retiro
28014 Madrid
Spain
museodelprado.es/en

The Prado Museum is a Spanish art museum. Many Spanish masterpieces are displayed in this gallery. Its vast collection includes 8,600 paintings and more than 700 sculptures.

Spain-USA Foundation

2801 16th St. NW
Washington, DC 20009
spainusafoundation.org

The Spain-USA Foundation, a nonprofit organization, supports Spanish cultural and educational activities to strengthen the relationship between the people of Spain and the United States.

SOURCE **NOTES**

CHAPTER 1. A TOUR OF SPAIN

1. "Palacio Real." *Lonely Planet*, n.d., lonelyplanet.com. Accessed 18 Dec. 2024.
2. "Palacio Real." *Frommer's*, n.d., frommers.com. Accessed 18 Dec. 2024.
3. "Collection." *Thyssen-Bornemisza Museo Nacional*, n.d., museothyssen.org. Accessed 18 Dec. 2024.
4 "Museo Nacional Centro de la Arte Reina Sofía." *Frommer's*, n.d., frommers.com. Accessed 18 Dec. 2024.
5. "Guernica." *Museo Reina Sofía*, n.d., museoreinasofia.es. Accessed 18 Dec. 2024.
6. Isabella Noble et al. *Spain*. Lonely Planet, 2023. 1717.
7. "Gran Vía." *Lonely Planet*, n.d., lonelyplanet.com. Accessed 18 Dec. 2024.
8. "Football Soccer Stadium Tour." *YouTube*, uploaded by Ultimate Bucket List, 14 Jan. 2024, youtube.com.
9. "Distance Madrid to Barcelona." *Distance Calculator*, n.d., distance.to. Accessed 18 Dec. 2024.
10. "Spain Cities by Population 2024." *World Population Review*, n.d., worldpopulationreview.com. Accessed 18 Dec. 2024.

CHAPTER 2. GEOGRAPHY

1. "Spain." *CIA World Factbook*, n.d., cia.gov. Accessed 18 Dec. 2024.
2. Richard John Harrison et al. "Spain." *Britannica*, 5 Jan. 2025, britannica.com. Accessed 6 Jan. 2025.
3. "Spain," *CIA World Factbook*.
4. "Spain," *CIA World Factbook*.
5. "Spain," *CIA World Factbook*.
6. "Spain," *CIA World Factbook*.
7. Harrison et al., "Spain."
8. Harrison et al., "Spain."
9. Vicente Rodriguez. "Sierra Nevada." *Britannica*, 14 Nov. 2024, britannica.com. Accessed 6 Jan. 2025.
10. "Highest Mountains in Spain." *World Atlas*, n.d., worldatlas.com. Accessed 18 Dec. 2024.
11. "Tagus River." *Britannica*, 13 Feb. 2023, britannica.com. Accessed 6 Jan. 2025.
12. "Guadiana River." *Britannica*, n.d., britannica.com. Accessed 6 Jan. 2025.
13. Stacey Leasca. "This Country Has the Most Clean Beaches in the World—and They're All Gorgeous." *Travel + Leisure*, 15 Aug. 2024, travelandleisure.com. Accessed 5 Jan. 2025.
14. Michael Shally-Jensen. *Countries, Peoples & Cultures: Western Europe*. Salem Press, 2015. 429.
15. Shally-Jensen, *Countries, Peoples & Cultures: Western Europe*, 429.
16. *Worldmark Encyclopedia of the Nations*. Gale, 2017. 731.
17. Constant Méheut. "Spain Bakes in Summer-Like Heat, and Worries about What Comes Next." *New York Times*, 28 Apr. 2023, nytimes.com. Accessed 6 Jan. 2025.
18. Stanley Reed and Rachel Chaundler. "Spain Is Thirsty. Here's How It Gets Water." *New York Times*, 12 Aug. 2024, nytimes.com. Accessed 6 Jan. 2025.

CHAPTER 3. PLANTS AND ANIMALS

1. "Geography of Spain." *La Moncloa*, n.d., lamoncloa.gob.es. Accessed 6 Jan. 2025.
2. "Geography of Spain."
3. "Geography of Spain."
4. "Geography of Spain."
5. "Spanish Imperial Eagle." *Animalia*, n.d., animalia.bio. Accessed 6 Jan. 2025.
6. "Tablas de Daimiel." *O España*, n.d., spain.info. Accessed 6 Jan. 2025.
7. "A Natural Wonder for Every Region of Spain." *O España*, n.d., spain.info. Accessed 6 Jan. 2025.
8. Rebecca Self. "Iberian Lynx Make a Remarkable Recovery in Portugal." *Natural Habitat Adventures*, 1 Nov. 2024, nathab.com. Accessed 6 Jan. 2025.
9. Sam Jones. "Iberian Lynx That Helped Save Species from Extinction Dies Aged 20." *Guardian*, 10 Nov. 2022, theguardian.com. Accessed 6 Jan. 2025.
10. "Spain's National Parks." *O España*, n.d., spain.info. Accessed 6 Jan. 2025.
11. Isabella Noble. "Tenerife's Most Beautiful National Park and Protected Areas, from Pine Forests to Volcanic Parks." *Lonely Planet*, 31 May 2022, lonelyplanet.com. Accessed 18 Dec. 2024.

CHAPTER 4. HISTORY

1. "Spain Country Profile." *BBC*, 21 Aug. 2023, bbc.com. Accessed 18 Dec. 2024.
2. Richard John Harrison et al. "Spain." *Britannica*, 5 Jan. 2025, britannica.com. Accessed 6 Jan. 2025.

CHAPTER 5. PEOPLE AND CULTURE

1. "Spain." *CIA World Factbook*, n.d., cia.gov. Accessed 6 Jan. 2025.
2. "Spain."
3. "Spain."
4. "Spain."
5. "San Lorenzo de El Escorial." *O España*, n.d., spain.info. Accessed 6 Jan. 2025.
6. "Miguel Induráin." *Olympics*, n.d., olympics.com. Accessed 6 Jan. 2025.
7. Juan Diego Madueño. "More Than Half Want to Limit or Ban Bulls and Hunting." *El Español*, 12 Jan. 2019, elespanol.com. Accessed 6 Jan. 2025.
8. Stephen Burgen. "Quiet Corridas: Spain Wonders What to Do with Unused Bullrings." *Guardian*, 21 Aug. 2022, theguardian.com. Accessed 6 Jan. 2025.
9. "Spain."

SOURCE **NOTES** CONTINUED

CHAPTER 6. POLITICS

1. "Spain Country Profile." *BBC*, 21 Aug. 2023, bbc.com. Accessed 18 Dec. 2024.
2. Richard John Harrison et al. "Spain." *Britannica*, 5 Jan. 2025, britannica.com. Accessed 6 Jan. 2025.
3. "Spain." *CIA World Factbook*, n.d., cia.gov. Accessed 6 Jan. 2025.
4. "Institutions of Spain." *La Moncloa*, n.d., lamoncloa.gob.es. Accessed 6 Jan. 2025.
5. Harrison et al., "Spain."

CHAPTER 7. ECONOMICS

1. Antonio Cazorla-Sánchez. "Spain." *World Book*, 31 July 2024, worldbookonline.com. Accessed 8 Aug. 2024.
2. *Worldmark Encyclopedia of the Nations.* Gale, 2017. 743.
3. "Agriculture." *La Moncloa*, n.d., lamoncloa.gob.es. Accessed 6 Jan. 2025.
4. *Worldmark Encyclopedia of the Nations*, 741.
5. Emilio Sánchez Hidalgo. "Why Does Spain Continue to Lead Europe in Unemployment?" *El Pais*, 2 Aug. 2023, english.elpais.com. Accessed 6 Jan. 2025.
6. Richard John Harrison et al. "Spain." *Britannica*, 5 Jan. 2025, britannica.com. Accessed 6 Jan. 2025.
7. "Spain." *CIA World Factbook*, n.d., cia.gov. Accessed 6 Jan. 2025.
8. Harrison et al., "Spain."
9. Cazorla-Sánchez, "Spain."
10. Harrison et al., "Spain."
11. "The 'Sol de Miró.'" *O España*, n.d., spain.info. Accessed 6 Jan. 2025.
12. "Mass Tourism Protesters Squirt Water at Barcelona Tourists." *BBC*, 7 July 2024, bbc.com. Accessed 18 Dec. 2024.
13. "Spain," *CIA World Factbook*.
14. "How to Get from Madrid to Barcelona by Train." *Eurail*, n.d., eurail.com. Accessed 27 Aug. 2024.

CHAPTER 8. SPAIN TODAY

1. "Spain Population." *Worldometer*, n.d., worldmeters.info. Accessed 6 Jan. 2025.
2. "Where Are the Largest Metropolitan Regions in the EU?" *Eurostat*, n.d., ec.europa.eu. Accessed 6 Jan. 2025.
3. *Worldmark Encyclopedia of the Nations.* Gale, 2017. 483.
4. *Worldmark Encyclopedia of the Nations*, 743.
5. "Spain." *CIA World Factbook*, n.d., cia.gov. Accessed 6 Jan. 2025.
6. "A Guide to Education & International Schools in Spain." *InterNations*, n.d., internations.org. Accessed 6 Jan. 2025.
7. Richard John Harrison et al. "Spain." *Britannica*, 5 Jan. 2025, britannica.com. Accessed 6 Jan. 2025.
8. *Worldmark Encyclopedia of the Nations*, 484.
9. "Spain's Christmas Lottery 'El Gordo' Starts Dishing Out Billions of Dollars in Prizes." *NPR*, 22 Dec. 2023, npr.org. Accessed 6 Jan. 2025.
10. "Spain." *Media Landscapes*, n.d., medialandscapes.org. Accessed 6 Jan. 2025.
11. "Spain," *CIA World Factbook*.

INDEX

ABOUT THE **AUTHOR**

LIZ SONNEBORN

A graduate of Swarthmore College, Liz Sonneborn has written more than 100 books for young readers and adults on a wide variety of subjects. Her specialties include American history, world history, biography, women's studies, and African American studies. She is the author of more than a dozen books about the history and culture of various countries, including Israel, Mexico, Canada, France, Iraq, Yemen, Kuwait, and Haiti.